JOURNEY
TO SUCCESS®

LEVEL
5

BUILDING BASIC SKILLS IN READING AND WRITING

New Readers Press®
ProLiteracy's publishing division

Journey to Success®: Building Basic Skills in Reading and Writing
Student Book 5
ISBN 978-1-944057-08-4

New Readers Press
ProLiteracy's Publishing Division
101 Wyoming Street, Syracuse, New York 13204
www.newreaderspress.com

Printed in the United States of America
10   9   8

Proceeds from the sale of New Readers Press materials support professional
development, training, and technical assistance programs of ProLiteracy
that benefit local literacy programs in the U.S. and around the globe.

Editorial Director: Terrie Lipke
Assistant Editor: Laura McLoughlin
Cover Design: Cathi Miller
Technology Specialist: Maryellen Casey

CONTENTS

LANGUAGE SKILLS MINI-LESSONS

UNIT 1

Work and Life Skills

Food for Thought

In this lesson, you will

READ

two passages about food:
- Be Smart at the Grocery Store
- Community Gardens

USE THIS READING SKILL

Recall key details

USE THIS VOCABULARY SKILL

Understand words with the prefix *trans-*

USE THIS WRITING SKILL

Write a procedural text

USE THESE KEY VOCABULARY WORDS

access the ability to use or get something

afford have enough money to pay for something

appeal to be pleasing or interesting to someone

budget a plan for spending money

display objects set up to show or advertise something

nutritious healthy; made up of things that a body needs

organize to arrange or order things

perimeter the outside edge or border

transform to change completely

transport to carry people or things from one place to another

UNDERSTAND THESE CONTENT VOCABULARY WORDS

agriculture the farming of plants or animals

aisle a row between shelves in a store where people walk

pollution the process of making air, water, or soil dirty

register a machine used in a store for calculating the total amount owed

Use the Vocabulary

Answer these questions about the vocabulary words. Use the definitions on page 8 to help you.

1. What kind of music **appeals** to you? Why?

   _____

2. Think of a **display** you have seen in a store or store window. What made you notice the **display**?

   _____

3. If you wanted to **transform** your home, what would you do?

   _____

4. Describe a **nutritious** meal.

   _____

5. What kinds of food do you have **access** to where you shop?

   _____

6. How can a **budget** help you? How is a city's **budget** different from a person's budget?

   _____

7. Describe the **perimeter** of the room you are in. How is it different from the center of the room?

   _____

8. How would you **transport** all the furniture in your house?

   _____

9. What are some ways you could **organize** your clothing?

   _____

10. What could you do if you couldn't **afford** your rent?

   _____

VOCABULARY TIP

Some words have more than one meaning. To figure out the correct meaning of the word, look for clues in the text.

Read these sentences and look for clues about the meaning of *display*. Then answer the questions.

*The bookstore has a **display** of cookbooks near the front door. There are several books about using fresh produce and a few about Mexican cooking.*

1. Which definition of *display* matches how the word is used in the sentence?
   a. *(verb)* to put something where people can see it
   b. *(verb)* to show that you have an emotion
   c. *(noun)* objects set up to show or advertise something
   d. *(noun)* the part of an electronic device that shows information

2. What clues helped you figure out the meaning? _____

Use Prior Knowledge

Before you read the article, look at the title, headings, and a few sentences to learn what the article will be about. Think about what you already know about the topic.

TIP
The headings tell what each part of the text will be about.

1. What will this article be about? _____

2. What do you already know about the topic? _____

3. What do you want to find out? _____

Take Notes

Take notes as you read. When you take notes, you think about what is important in the text. Your notes can help you answer questions later. You can make notes in the margin or underline and circle important details in the text.

Read the passage. As you read, makes notes in the margin and in the text.

Be Smart at the Grocery Store

1 Are you smart when you shop for food? It's easy to spend too much money and buy unneeded things at the grocery store. But some planning and knowledge can help you buy what you need, make healthy choices, and get the best prices.

Plan Before You Go

Underline things you should do before going to the store.

2 Smart shopping starts before you get to the store. Start by planning your meals for the week. To save money, clip coupons and check sale ads. Then make a list of what you need. Before you shop, **organize** your food cabinets and drawers. Check what you already have so that you don't buy unneeded items.

3 Before you shop, know your food **budget**. You may want to bring cash to the store and leave credit cards at home. That way, you can't overspend. Finally, make sure you eat before shopping. Hungry shoppers buy things that aren't on their lists.

Understand the Store

4 An average grocery store has more than 38,000 items. It's helpful to understand how a store is set up and how stores get you to buy and spend more.

Make a note about where you can find healthy foods. Underline examples in paragraph 5.

5 For healthy foods, shop on the **perimeter** of the store. This is where stores keep fresh fruits and vegetables, milk, eggs, meat, and fish. The middle aisles often have junk food and packaged food. Stores often put things shoppers need the most— like milk and eggs—on the back wall. This makes shoppers walk through the center aisles, where they might pick up things they don't need.

Make a note about how items are placed on shelves.

6 Stores place products carefully. A product's location on a shelf is important. The most expensive products usually go at eye level, where you will see them first. Less expensive items go on the top and bottom shelves. Foods that **appeal** to kids are often at their eye level.

7 Endcaps are another key spot for product placement. These are **displays** at the end of aisles that are easy to see. But if these products aren't on your list, keep going. Another popular spot is the area around the registers. Stores make a lot of money on items like candy bars and magazines in the checkout area. A shopper spends about 3 minutes 11 seconds in line, so it's easy to buy something you don't need.

8 When you shop for food, it's best to plan ahead, stick to your list, and be kind to your wallet.

Check Your Comprehension

Answer these questions about the article.

1. What is this article mostly about? _____

HINT
The headings tell main topics of the text.

2. How are items arranged on the shelves in a grocery store? _____

_____

3. Look at the diagram. What does it show you? _____

_____

Recall Key Details

After you read informational text, you should be able to recall details and examples to answer questions about the text. Think about the answers to questions such as Who? What? When? Where? Why? How?

Answer the questions using details from the article.

1. According to the article, what are the two main things you can do to be a better shopper?

   a. _____

   b. _____

2. According to the article, why should you check your food cabinets and drawers?

   _____

3. According to paragraph 3, why should you eat before grocery shopping?

   _____

4. What is one thing you can do so that you don't overspend on food? _____

5. Where can you find healthy foods in a grocery store? _____

6. What are some examples of these healthier foods? _____

7. What are three examples of how stores place products to sell more and make more money?

   _____

8. How long does a shopper spend in line? _____ What can happen in that time?

   _____

 IMPROVE YOUR READING

Practice reading paragraph 1 of "Be Smart at the Grocery Store" silently. Then read it again, paying attention to punctuation and grouping words into phrases. Then take turns with a partner reading the paragraph aloud.

Practice the Skills

Preview the passage and think about what you already know about the topic. Answer the questions.

1. Read the title. What will this passage be about? _____

2. What do you already know about the topic? _____

3. What do you want to find out about the topic? _____

_____

Take notes as you read the article. Complete the prompts in the margin.

Community Gardens

Underline the definition of *community garden.*

1   Many people have a hard time buying healthy food, like fresh fruits and vegetables. According to the U.S. Department of Agriculture, about 18 million Americans live in food deserts. Food deserts are communities without **access** to fresh, healthy food at a price people can **afford**. For people in cities, community gardens can help. A community garden is a piece of land shared by a group of people to grow fresh produce. These gardens can benefit the people who garden, the environment, and the entire community.

Improving Health

2   Community gardens can give people a place to grow their own healthy food. Some studies show that community gardeners have healthier diets than people who do not garden. Their families eat more **nutritious** fruits and vegetables. And it is free or low cost.

3   There are other health benefits besides a better diet. Community gardens get people outdoors and moving. Gardening is a good form of exercise. Being outdoors can also improve mental health. Gardens can be relaxing and quiet places away from the noise of a city.

Improving the Environment

Underline details about how produce travels to stores.

4   Community gardens can help the environment. In the United States, fresh produce travels an average of 1,500 miles from a farm to your plate. The trucks, trains, boats, and planes that **transport** food all cause pollution. Produce often takes 7 to 14 days to reach a store. Almost half of it spoils during that time. Food grown in a community garden doesn't create pollution or cause waste.

5   Community gardens also help the local environment. The plants add oxygen to the air and lower air pollution. The soil holds rainwater. These green spaces also offer food to birds and insects like bees and butterflies.

Improving Communities

Write notes about how gardens help communities.

6   Community gardens can also improve whole communities. Many community gardens are planted on unused land. A garden can **transform** a trash-filled lot into a beautiful green space. This can help people feel pride and ownership in their community. Often, property values increase near community gardens.

7   Gardens are a place for neighbors to meet and share information. They are good places to teach children about where food comes from. Many community gardens also give back. Gardeners may give extra food to food banks or to people in need.

An unused lot in Detroit, Michigan, was transformed into a community garden.

Check Your Comprehension

Answer these questions about the article.

1. What is a community garden? _____

2. What are the three main things that a community garden can improve? _____

_____

3. What can you tell from the two photos? _____

_____

Practice Recalling Key Details

Key details in a text can help you answer questions about who, what, when, where, why, and how.

Reread paragraph 1. Answer the questions with key details from the text.

1. What is a food desert? _____

2. How many people live in food deserts? _____

3. Who can benefit from a community garden? _____

Sometimes a text will give several important details about a topic. A graphic organizer can help you record these details from the text. Then you can use the information in the graphic organizer to draw conclusions.

Use the graphic organizer to record details from paragraph 4 about how food travels in the United States. Then answer the questions based on the details you recorded.

DETAILS ABOUT HOW FOOD GETS FROM THE FARM TO YOUR TABLE			
4.	5.	6.	7.

8. Based on the details from the text, what can you tell about how food gets from a farm to your table?

_____

9. How does a community garden address the problem? _____

_____

 IMPROVE YOUR READING

Listen as your teacher reads paragraphs 2 and 3 of "Community Gardens." Pay attention to your teacher's tone and expression. Then read the paragraphs aloud with your teacher.

Respond to the Readings

Answer these questions about the articles.

1. What is the main point of the article "Be Smart at the Grocery Store"? _____

    _____

2. Which specific ideas from the article "Be Smart at the Grocery Store" could help you be a better shopper?

    _____

3. What is the main point of the article "Community Gardens"? _____

    _____

HINT
Think about what the article is mostly about and look at the headings.

4. Which benefits of a community garden would you be likely to see first? Which benefits probably take years?

    _____

5. How are the two articles similar and different? _____

    _____

Use Word Parts: Prefix *trans-*

The prefix *trans-* means "across" or "through." You can use what you know about word parts to help you figure out the meaning of words. For example, in the word *transport*, the prefix *trans-* means "across" and the root *port* means "carry." *Transport* means "carry across."

TIP
Try to divide words into parts to figure out their meaning. For example, what parts of the words transaction and transplant do you know?

Complete each sentence with a word from the box. Use a dictionary if you don't know the meaning of a word.

transaction	transfer	translate	transplant	transportation

1. There isn't enough money in my checking account, so I need to _____ some money from my savings account.

2. When the tomato plants get 6 inches tall, you should _____ them to a larger pot or to the garden.

3. I cannot speak Spanish, but my children can. They _____ for me when we visit Mexico.

4. If you live in a big city, you might have many _____ choices, like buses, taxis, cars, and trains.

5. Ken writes down each _____ in his checkbook so he knows how much money is in his account.

Write your own sentences using these words. Use a dictionary if you need to.

6. transparent _____

7. transmit _____

Review the Vocabulary

Circle the letter of the answer that best completes the sentence.

1. If you wanted to eat some **nutritious** food, you would probably have _____.
   a. fresh fruits and vegetables
   b. chocolate cake with ice cream
   c. a bag of chips and a can of soda

2. If you walk on the **perimeter** of a store, you are walking _____.
   a. around the edge
   b. up and down the aisles
   c. near the entrance

3. If a food **appeals** to you, it is a food that you _____.
   a. never ate before
   b. eat daily
   c. like to eat

4. If you **organize** your clothing, you _____.
   a. throw it away
   b. put it in order
   c. wash it

Complete each sentence with a word from the box.

access	afford	appeal	budget	display
nutritious	organize	perimeter	transformed	transport

5. Maggie created a _____ so she knew how much money she could spend at the mall.

6. The living room used to be very dark, but we _____ it by painting the walls and removing the old carpet.

7. Ray wants to buy a new car, but he can't _____ it right now.

8. The museum has a _____ of old coins and other objects from a ship that sank in the 1700s.

9. Students and teachers will need a key if they need _____ to the building after 9 p.m.

10. The football team uses a private jet to _____ players and equipment to out-of-state games.

Write two new sentences. Use a word from the box in each sentence.

11. _____

_____

12. _____

_____

Write a Procedural Text

A procedural text tells readers how to make something or do something. Procedural text tells you what to do and the order in which you should do it. You've probably seen many examples of procedural texts. For example, a manual that tells how to program your TV, an online article about fixing a car, a recipe, and directions for a science experiment are all examples of procedural texts.

A procedural text should include:

- ✓ A sentence that explains the purpose of your text
- ✓ Headings that organize your information
- ✓ Steps given in the correct order
- ✓ Words and phrases that show time order
- ✓ A concluding sentence that relates to your ideas

Read the prompt.

> Write a procedural text instructing someone how to be a smart shopper at the grocery store. Organize your ideas and put them in a logical order. Use information from your own experiences, this lesson, and additional internet research to support your ideas.

Plan Your Writing

Before you begin writing, think about what information you want to give your reader. Think about what a reader needs to know in order to be a smart shopper. Use the graphic organizer to organize your ideas. Use headings to break the ideas into groups. Put your ideas in the correct order.

How to _____
_____
(introductory sentence or paragraph explaining what you will be instructing someone to do)
(heading 1)
(steps)
(steps)
(heading 2)
(steps)
(steps)
(conclusion sentence or paragraph)

Write Your Procedural Text

On the lines below or on a computer, write your procedural text.

_____

_____

_____

_____

_____

_____

_____

_____

Review Your Writing

Use this list to check your writing.

- [ ] My first sentence tells the topic I am writing about.
- [ ] I organized my ideas.
- [ ] I put the steps in time order.
- [ ] I used time order words and phrases.
- [ ] I checked the spelling and punctuation.

For practice with sentence fragments, complete the Language Skills Mini-Lesson on page 135.

After you check your work, make any corrections. Read your text aloud to a partner. Then discuss how your procedural texts were similar and different.

Think and Discuss

Everyone needs to eat. However, food security is a problem for many people in the United States. The U.S. Department of Agriculture says being food secure means having "access, at all times, to enough food for an active, healthy life for all household members." In 2016, about 15.6 million U.S. households were not food secure. This means they did not have enough food to meet their needs.

Why do you think food security is a problem? What do you think could be done to solve the problem? Talk about the questions in small groups.

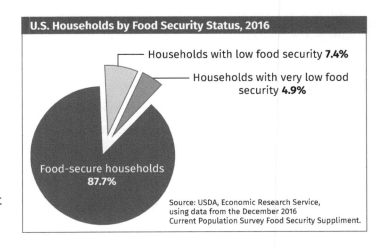

U.S. Households by Food Security Status, 2016

Households with low food security **7.4%**

Households with very low food security **4.9%**

Food-secure households **87.7%**

Source: USDA, Economic Research Service, using data from the December 2016 Current Population Survey Food Security Suppliment.

Job Hunting Strategies

In this lesson, you will

READ

two passages about job hunting strategies:
- How to Hunt for a Job
- Work Your Way to a Full-Time Job

USE THIS READING SKILL

Identify reasons and evidence

USE THIS VOCABULARY SKILL

The prefix *con-*

USE THIS WRITING SKILL

Write a cover letter

USE THESE KEY VOCABULARY WORDS

accomplish to complete a task or reach a goal

advantage something that helps one person succeed over another

consider to think carefully about something to make a good decision

convince to get somebody to agree with you

efficient doing something well without wasting time or energy

obvious easy to understand or see

productive getting a lot done

profile a description of a person that gives useful information

respond to answer or reply to something

strategy a plan to reach a goal

UNDERSTAND THESE CONTENT VOCABULARY WORDS

internship a work position, sometimes paid and sometimes not, in which a person learns on the job

networking sharing information with people you know

refer to send somebody to a person or place for a specific purpose

résumé a document that shows a worker's experience, skills, and education

Use the Vocabulary

Answer these questions about the vocabulary words. Use the definitions on page 18 to help you.

1. What is something that you **accomplished** this week? How did you **accomplish** it?

    _____

2. Would you **consider** volunteering at a neighborhood school? Explain why or why not.

    _____

3. How would you **respond** to an invitation to a friend's wedding?

    _____

4. Which is more **efficient** for you—typing on the computer or writing with a pen? Explain.

    _____

5. When job hunting, do you think knowing a lot of people is an **advantage**? Explain.

    _____

6. How can you make your feelings and emotions **obvious** to other people?

    _____

7. What would a **productive** day be like for you?

    _____

8. What information should a person put on a social media **profile**?

    _____

9. How would you **convince** a friend to go the movies with you?

    _____

10. What **strategy** would you use if you wanted to make more money?

    _____

VOCABULARY TIP

To figure out the meaning of a word you don't know, look for clues in the text. An author might use a synonym, or a word with similar meaning, in nearby sentences.

Read these sentences. Look for clues that help you figure out the meaning of *respond*. Then answer the question.

*Kelly works at a call center. The workers try to **respond** to calls from customers within 15 minutes. During busy times, though, it may be 60 minutes before they can answer questions.*

What word from the sentences means about the same as *respond*? _____

Preview

When you preview informational text, you should read the title and headings. Also look at photos or other visual elements and read the captions.

1. Based on the title, what will this article be about? _____

2. What are the headings in the article? _____

3. What does the photo show? _____

Monitor Understanding

As you read, think about what you are learning. Stop and ask yourself questions. Then you can look for the answers. This will help you pay attention as you read.

Read the article. Answer the questions in the margin. The first one is an example of a question a reader might ask.

Sample question: How have strategies changed?

What questions do you have about job hunting in the past?

What question do you have about job search websites?

What question do you have about networking websites?

How to Hunt for a Job

1 **Strategies** for finding a job have changed a lot from 25 years ago. In the past, employers and job seekers connected through newspaper ads and help wanted signs. Today, job seekers and employers frequently connect online. They use job search websites, online networking sites, and community job centers to find work.

A woman uses a computer at a community job center.

2 Ads and help wanted signs were not an **efficient** way to find a job. Newspaper ads had only a short description of the job. A job seeker would need to print and mail a résumé and cover letter. An employer might take several weeks to **respond**, if they responded at all. Looking for help wanted signs was also not very efficient. It depended a lot on being in the right place at the right time.

3 There are many **advantages** to online job hunting. It helps job seekers **accomplish** their goals sooner. They can look at many job listings. They can connect with a lot of different people, and they can apply for jobs online.

Job Search Websites

4 A job search website lists jobs from many employers. These sites benefit employers because they can reach a lot of people quickly and easily. Employers can include detailed descriptions of the job and list the skills job seekers should have. They can also give information about the company.

5 These sites also benefit job seekers. They can learn about local jobs or jobs in other cities. Workers can see which jobs match their experience and goals. They can get enough information about the job to decide if it's worth applying for. And they can apply for a job immediately.

Networking Websites

6 A business networking website is a way for people with similar career goals to connect. Workers can post **profiles** with information about their education, skills, and work experience. Workers can use their profiles to be seen by employers. Employers use the profiles to look for good workers.

Community Job Centers

7 Community job centers are a great resource for job hunters. These centers often work with local employers and can refer workers to available jobs. Most centers also offer training for using computers and other job skills. They can help you write a résumé or complete an application.

Check Your Comprehension

Answer these questions about the article.

1. How did workers look for jobs in the past? _____

2. What are three ways workers today can look for jobs, according to the article? _____

   _____

3. Who benefits from job search websites? _____

   _____

Identify Reasons and Evidence

In informational texts, authors use reasons and evidence to support their points, or claims. Strong reasons and evidence help the readers agree that the points are true.

Answer the questions with reasons and evidence from the text.

1. In the first sentence of paragraph 1, what point or claim does the author make? _____

   _____

2. What reasons and evidence does the author use to support this point? _____

   _____

3. In paragraph 2, how does the author support the point that ads and help wanted signs were inefficient?

   _____

4. In paragraph 3, what advantages to online job hunting are given? _____

   _____

5. What point does the author make in paragraph 4? _____

   _____

6. What reasons and evidence support this point? _____

   _____

> **TIP**
> The word *because* is a very common signal that an author is giving a reason to support a point.

7. Which of these supports the point that job seekers benefit from job search websites? Circle all that apply.
   a. Workers can get detailed information about jobs.
   b. Workers can apply immediately for jobs they are interested in.
   c. Workers can see a lot of job listings that aren't useful to them.
   d. Workers may not hear back from employers after they apply for jobs.

 IMPROVE YOUR READING

Practice reading paragraph 3 of "How to Hunt for a Job" silently. The first time you read, try to sound out long or difficult words. Read the paragraph several times, focusing on your speed. Try to read as fast as you talk. After you have practiced reading on your own, take turns reading the paragraph aloud with a partner.

Practice the Skills

Preview the article. Answer the questions.

1. Read the title. What will this article be about? _____

2. Look at the headings. What kinds of work will this article discuss?

   _____

3. Look at the photo and read the caption. What is the photo about? _____

TIP
This article has both headings and subheadings.

Read the article. As you read, pause to ask yourself questions and find the answers.

Work Your Way to a Full-Time Job

What questions do you have about finding other work opportunities?

1 Most people who are looking for work are looking for full-time jobs. However, if you are out of work and it is taking a while to find a full-time job, you should **consider** other work opportunities. With volunteering, an internship, or a part-time job, you may be able to work your way to a full-time job.

2 There are several reasons to stay busy if you are currently between jobs. By volunteering, interning, or working part-time, you can:

- Close the gap. If you are not working, there is a "job gap" on your resume or application. This is a period of unemployment. Employers do not like job gaps. They wonder why you haven't been working.

- Network. Even if you don't work full time, you can network with others. In other words, you can build work connections that may lead to the job you want.

- Build job skills. Volunteering, interning, or working part time can help you stay current with the skills you already have. You can also learn new skills and practice good teamwork.

- Improve your mental health. Unemployed people are more likely than full-time workers to suffer from depression. Staying busy and **productive** reduces depression.

Volunteer Work

What questions do you have about using volunteer work to find a full-time job?

3 Volunteering, which is unpaid work to help others, might seem like a bad idea when you need money. However, volunteering can help you in all the ways listed above and help your community. It is also a chance to explore a new line of work.

Internships

What questions do you have about finding an internship?

4 Another kind of work opportunity that can lead to a full-time job is an internship in your field or industry. An internship is on-the-job-training. Most internships last from two to six months. Some interns get paid. Some do not. Either way, you can gain work experience and build connections in your field.

Volunteering improves work skills and helps you make work-related connections.

iStock.com/Wavebreakmedia

Part-Time Work

5 Perhaps the most **obvious** solution to unemployment is a part-time job. Part-time jobs are not only ideal for making some money when you are unemployed, but if the job is in your industry, all the better. Many companies hire their part-time employees first when a full-time job becomes available.

6 Are you **convinced**? Struggling to find a full-time job doesn't mean you can't find work! Volunteering, taking an internship, or working at a part-time job can help you move closer to your job goal.

Check Your Comprehension

Answer these questions about the passage.

1. According to paragraph 1 in the article, what should workers do instead of waiting around for a full-time job?

   _____

2. What are the three main work opportunities discussed in the article? _____

   _____

3. What is volunteer work? _____

Practice Identifying Reasons and Evidence

Authors support their ideas by giving reasons and evidence. You can use a graphic organizer to record the author's claim, or point, and the supporting reasons and evidence. You can analyze the reasons and evidence to judge whether the author has proved his or her point.

HINT
In this article, the author uses the word *reasons* to support the claim.

Complete the graphic organizer below. Then answer the questions.

THE AUTHOR'S CLAIM OR POINT
1.

REASON/EVIDENCE	REASON/EVIDENCE	REASON/EVIDENCE	REASON/EVIDENCE
2.	3.	4.	5.

6. In paragraph 3, what additional reasons does the author give for volunteering?

   _____

7. What is an additional benefit to getting an internship? _____

8. Based on the reasons and evidence in the article, do you think there is support for the author's claim? Explain your answer.

   _____

 IMPROVE YOUR READING

Listen and read along silently as your teacher reads the list of bullets in paragraph 2 of the article "Work Your Way to a Full-Time Job." Notice where your teacher pauses. Then read the list aloud with your teacher, pausing or slowing down when your teacher does.

Respond to the Readings

Answer these questions about the articles.

HINT
Look at paragraphs 1 and 2 of "New Ways to Hunt for a Job."

1. Why might it have been harder to find the right job in the past?

   _____

2. Which strategy for job hunting from "How to Hunt for a Job" do you think works best? Explain.

   _____

3. What are some differences between internships, volunteer work, and part-time jobs?

   _____

4. Do you think volunteer work, an internship, or a part-time job is the best solution for someone who is between jobs? Explain your answer.

   _____

5. How are the two articles in this lesson similar? How does the advice they give differ?

   _____

Use Word Parts: Prefix con-

Knowing the meaning of roots, prefixes, and suffixes can help you figure out the meaning of words. The prefix con- can mean either "with" or "thoroughly." For example, the word connect means "to link together." The word conclude means "thoroughly finished."

TIP
Remember the prefix con- has two meanings—"with" and "thoroughly." When trying to figure out the meaning of a con- word, try both meanings.

Complete each sentence with a word from the box. Use a dictionary if you don't know the meaning of a word.

conclude	conflict	consequences	consistent	contour

1. After reading all the articles online, I can _____ that I need a new stove.

2. If you drive over the speed limit, there are _____ like tickets, fines, and the loss of your driver's license.

3. I have a schedule _____ on Monday morning. I am supposed to go to a dentist appointment and take my car into the shop.

4. If you want to lose weight, be _____ with your diet and exercise plan. You can't just follow it part of the time.

5. From 10 miles away, you can see the _____, or curve, of the earth.

Write your own sentences using these words. Use a dictionary if you need to.

6. confess _____

7. confusion _____

Review the Vocabulary

Circle the letter of the answer that best completes the sentence.

1. If you want to **accomplish** a goal, you should
    _____.

    a. start over with something new

    b. give up

    c. make a little progress every day

2. If a person is **productive**, that person _____.

    a. is funny

    b. gets a lot done

    c. needs a new job

3. If you are **considering** doing something, you
    would _____.

    a. refuse to do it

    b. do something very quickly

    c. think about it carefully

4. If a car is **efficient**, it _____.

    a. looks really nice

    b. breaks down a lot

    c. does not use much gas

Complete each sentence with a word from the box.

accomplish	advantage	consider	convince	efficient
obvious	productive	profile	respond	strategy

5. When a baby cries, most parents _____ by checking to see if the baby is OK.

6. Being tall is usually an _____ for a basketball player.

7. My son wants to go to the concert, but first he must _____ me that it's a good idea.

8. In her social media _____, she shares information about her life.

9. Her _____ for losing weight is to eat less and exercise more.

10. He is wearing a cast on his leg from his toes to his hip. It is _____ to everyone that his leg is broken.

Write two new sentences. Use a word from the box in each sentence.

11. _____

    _____

12. _____

    _____

Write a Cover Letter

A cover letter (or email) is sent with your resume or application when you are applying for a job. You may think that your resume already has all the information an employer needs. But a cover letter allows you to introduce yourself to the employer. It lets you make an argument about why you should be hired. And it is a great place for you to include reasons and evidence to support your claim that you should be hired.

A cover letter should include:

- ✔ A sentence that tells the position you are applying for
- ✔ A statement about why you are a good match for the job
- ✔ Sentences that give examples of your related work experience, skills, education, and training
- ✔ A concluding sentence that summarizes your letter and encourages the employer to contact you

Read the prompt.

> Think of a job you would like to have. Write a cover letter to the employer describing why the employer should hire you. Include evidence and examples of your related work experience, skills, education, and training.

Plan Your Writing

Before you begin writing, think about how the employer looks at job applicants. What are the employer's most urgent needs? You want to convince the employer you can meet these needs. You will do this with reasons and evidence. In this case the reasons and evidence are your experience, skills, training, and education.

Use the graphic organizer to plan your letter.

Dear Mr. / Ms. _____ :
(greeting)

_____
(First paragraph: Sentence about the job you are applying for)

_____
(Middle paragraphs: Examples and evidence of why you are a good match, such as experience, skills, and education)

_____

_____

_____
(Concluding sentence or paragraph: Thank the employer, summarize your letter, and encourage them to contact you.)

_____

Write Your Cover Letter

On the lines below or on a computer, write your cover letter.

_____

_____

_____

_____

_____

_____

_____

_____

_____

> **TIP**
>
> A cover letter should start with a formal greeting, such as: *Dear Mr. / Ms. [last name]* or *Dear Hiring Manager.*

Review Your Writing

Use this list to check your writing.

- ☐ Each sentence expresses a complete thought.
- ☐ I named the job I was applying for.
- ☐ I gave evidence and examples about my experience, skills, training, and education.
- ☐ I wrote a conclusion.
- ☐ I checked the spelling and punctuation.

After you check your work, make any corrections. Read your cover letter aloud to a partner. Then discuss what you learned about each others' job skills and work experience, skills, education, and training.

Think and Discuss

Another way to get a job is to create one. In other words, you could start your own business. This can work well for some people but not so well for others.

iStock.com/ygajic

- What are some reasons to start a business?

- What are some reasons not to start a business?

- What are some challenges people probably have when they start their own business?

Talk about the questions in small groups. Would you consider starting your own business?

Decisions, Decisions

In this lesson, you will

READ
two articles about:
- Making Good Decisions
- Credit Card or Debit Card?

USE THIS READING SKILL
Understand cause and effect

USE THIS VOCABULARY SKILL
Understand words with the suffix *-ic*

USE THIS WRITING SKILL
Write a narrative paragraph

USE THESE KEY VOCABULARY WORDS
adjust to make small changes to something to improve it

appropriate what is correct or right for a particular time, situation, or purpose

borrow to take and use something for a short time before returning it

consequences the results of something that happens

evaluate to think carefully about something to form an opinion about it

limit a maximum amount

loan money that is borrowed or lent

specific certain and exact; particular

transfer to move from one person or place to another

values your beliefs about what is right and wrong or about what is important

UNDERSTAND THESE CONTENT VOCABULARY WORDS
balance the amount of money you owe

interest the money you are charged if you borrow money

overdraft when you take more money out of your bank account than is available

point of sale the place where a purchase is made

terms and conditions the rules that you agree to follow when you get a credit or debit card

transaction a business deal; when goods, services, or money are passed from one person, account, etc., to another

Use the Vocabulary

Answer these questions about the vocabulary words. Use the definitions on page 28 to help you.

1. Describe two things that have a **limit**.

   _____

2. Could you be friends with someone who has different **values** from yours? Explain your answer.

   _____

3. Name two places where what is considered **appropriate** clothing is different.

   _____

4. When is it important to **evaluate** how you're doing at work, home, or school?

   _____

5. Describe a time you had to **adjust** to something different or new.

   _____

6. Describe something that has to be done at a **specific** time or place.

   _____

7. Is it better to **borrow** money to buy something you want or to wait until you can pay for it yourself? Explain.

   _____

8. What are the **consequences** of getting to school or work late?

   _____

9. What are two things you can **transfer**?

   _____

10. Is it a good idea to give a friend a **loan**? Why or why not?

   _____

VOCABULARY TIP

Some words, like *limit* and *values*, have more than one meaning. To figure out the correct meaning, think about how the word is being used. Ask yourself, for example, is this word a noun or a verb?

Read the three definitions of *values*. Read the sentences. Write the letter of the definition that matches how *values* is used in each.

a. beliefs about what is right and wrong

b. estimates the worth of

c. thinks highly of

_____ **1.** Jarrod *values* his bike at $150.

_____ **2.** Stella *values* her co-workers' opinion.

_____ **3.** Mario wants to meet a woman who has similar *values* to his.

Set a Purpose for Reading

When you set a purpose for reading, you understand more of what you read. Before you read, skim the article to find out what you will be learning. Then, ask yourself what you can expect to learn from this article.

1. What will this article be about? _____

2. What do you already know about the topic? _____

3. What can you expect to learn? _____

Make Connections

When you make connections, you find ways to connect what you read with your own experiences. As you read, ask yourself if anything in this article relates to your own life. This will help you better understand what you read.

Read the article. Check that you understand what you are reading. Answer the questions in the margin as you read.

Making Good Decisions

1 Decisions are choices you make about something after thinking about it for a while. Some decisions are easy (what you should wear). Some are a little more difficult (if you should get married). Decision making is personal. It's about recognizing what's important to you. There are no right answers. However, there are steps you can follow to make decisions that represent your **values**.

Does this remind you of anything in your own life?

Step 1: Identify a decision you need to make. Your decision should be clear and **specific**.

Step 2: Collect facts and information that are directly related to the decision. Talk to people who have had to make a similar decision. Get their advice and learn from their experiences. Go online and learn as much as you can about the topic. Then, make a list of all possible options, even the ones that seem a little silly.

Step 4: Trust yourself to make the decision that is best for you. Because you've done everything you can to make a good decision, you shouldn't be afraid that you made the wrong choice. If you don't act on what you want, there is no point in making the decision in the first place.

What does Step 3 make you think of?

Step 3: List the options in order, based on your values. Imagine what it would be like if you carried out each choice. Ask yourself, *What's the worst thing that could happen? Will I be comfortable living with the **consequences***? As you do this, you'll see that some options are more likely to help you reach your goal than others.

Step 5: Review your decision. **Evaluate** the results. Ask yourself how you feel about your choice. You may want to make some changes, **adjust** your choice, or go back a step or two. With practice, you'll become more comfortable with the decision-making process.

Check Your Comprehension

Answer these questions about the article.

1. What makes decision making personal? _____

2. What research can you do to help you make a decision? _____

3. Why should you review your decision? _____

Understand Cause and Effect

Cause and effect connects two events. The cause tells you why something happened. An effect tells you what happened as a result of the cause. Signal words and phrases like those in the box below can help you determine what causes something to happen.

as a result	because	consequently	due to	for this reason	if
in order to	since	so	then	therefore	when

1. Reread Step 2. Which sentence shows a cause and effect based on the text? Circle the letter.

   a. Talk to people who have had to make a similar decision in order to learn from their experiences.
   b. As a result, it will help you come up with possible options.
   c. Make a list of all possible choices, even the ones that seem a little silly.

Combine the sentences. Use the signal word or phrase in parentheses to connect them.

2. There are no right answers. Decision making is personal. (because)

   _____

3. You imagine the results of each option. You'll see that some options are more likely to help you reach your goal. (if)

   _____

4. You will make a good decision. Research your options online. (consequently)

   _____

   > **HINT**
   > Ask yourself which is the cause and which is the effect. It may help you to swap the order of the sentences.

5. Review your decision. Make better decisions in the future. (in order to)

   _____

6. You spent a long time making the decision. Act on it. (for that reason)

   _____

 Fluency   **IMPROVE YOUR READING**

Practice reading the steps for "Making Good Decisions" silently. In a group of three, take turns reading each tip aloud. Pay attention to your expression and tone as you read.

Practice the Skills

Set a purpose for reading. Answer the questions.

1. Skim the article. What will you be learning about? _____

2. What do you already know about the topic? _____

3. What should be your purpose for reading this article? _____

Read the article. As you read, use the prompts in the margin to help you make personal connections to the text.

Credit Card or Debit Card?

Can you relate to choosing between a credit card and a debit card?

1   It's important to understand the **appropriate** ways to use credit cards and debit cards so you can choose the best card for you.

Credit Cards

2   Credit cards are like a **loan** that you can use to buy things and pay them off over time. There is a **limit** on how much money the bank or credit card company will let you borrow on the account. The limit is based on your credit history.

3   Anything charged to your credit card is added to your balance. Consequently, you add to your balance every time you swipe your card, and you lower it every time you make a payment.

Do you know if you have good credit?

4   Every month you pay back some or all of the money you **borrow**. If you don't pay the full balance, you will be charged interest. In order to build a good credit history, keep your balance to an amount you can repay in full each month.

5   It's important to understand the terms and conditions of your credit card. Some banks charge a fee if you get a cash advance, make a late payment, or go over your credit limit. For this reason, review your monthly statements and call customer service if you have any questions.

Debit Cards

6   Debit cards are linked directly to your checking account. You can use them anywhere credit cards are accepted and at ATMs when you need to get cash, deposit checks, transfer between accounts, or see your account balances. You can often get cash from your account at a point of sale.

7   The money you spend when you use a debit card is not a loan. Therefore, there are no monthly payments, late fees, or interest charges. When you swipe your card, the money is **transferred** directly out of your account.

8   Using debit cards won't help build your credit history. You can use only as much money as you have in your account. If you try to withdraw more money than you have in your account, the transaction will be declined. As a result, debit cards work well for people who worry that they will overspend with a credit card or who have bad credit.

9   It can be difficult to keep track of your account balance with a debit card. If you aren't paying attention, you might spend more money than you have available. When this happens, your bank may charge an overdraft fee.

Check Your Comprehension

Answer these questions about the article.

1. How do banks decide on your credit limit? _____

2. What happens to your balance when you make a payment on your credit card? _____

3. What is the consequence of not paying back the full amount you owe on your credit card each month?

   _____

Practice Understanding Cause and Effect

Reread the section on credit cards in the article. Match each cause on the left with its correct effect on the right. Then use a signal word or phrase from the box to rewrite each pair as a new sentence.

1. _____ You make a purchase.

2. _____ You don't pay off your balance.

3. _____ You go over your credit limit.

4. _____ You make a payment.

a. You reduce your balance.

b. You will be charged interest.

c. You add to your balance.

d. You pay a fee.

HINT
To find the cause, ask "Why does it happen?"
To find the effect, ask "What happens?"

as a result	because	consequently	due to	for this reason	if
in order to	since	so	then	therefore	when

5. _____

6. _____

7. _____

8. _____

Sometimes different effects can be produced by a single cause.

Reread the section Debit Cards in the article. Then complete the graphic organizer with the possible effects.

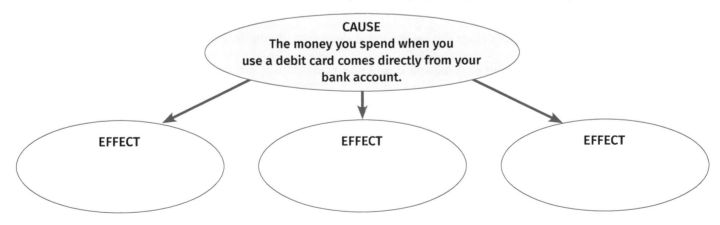

CAUSE
The money you spend when you use a debit card comes directly from your bank account.

EFFECT

EFFECT

EFFECT

Fluency   **IMPROVE YOUR READING**

Read paragraph 6 of "Credit Card or Debit Card?" silently. As you read, pause at punctuation marks like commas and periods. Work with a partner. Take turns reading one sentence at a time.

Respond to the Readings

Answer these questions about the articles.

1. Why should you be specific when you need to make a decision? _____

2. What is the connection between using your feelings and using your values when making a decision?
   a. Your values are the same as your feelings.
   b. If your decision represents your values, it probably feels right to you.
   c. If you value something, you won't care how you feel about your decision.

3. Why should you review your credit card statement carefully? _____
   _____

4. Why doesn't using a debit card help build your credit history? _____
   _____

5. What advice would you give a friend who is trying to decide if she needs a credit card, a debit card, or both?
   _____

Use Word Parts: Suffix -ic

The suffix -ic means "having characteristics of." You can add -ic to the end of some nouns or verbs to make adjectives. For example, when you add the suffix -ic to the noun hero, the new word is the adjective heroic.

HINT
If a word ends in e or y, drop the vowel before you add -ic. For example: specify → specific.

Add the suffix -ic to the nouns in the first column. Use a dictionary to check your spelling.

	+ -ic
1. artist	
2. athlete	
3. base	

	+ -ic
4. economy	
5. electron	
6. history	

Complete each sentence with a word from the boxes. Use a dictionary if you don't know the meaning of a word.

7. Choosing the right credit or debit card for you is an important _____ decision.

8. You can use _____ banking to transfer money using your computer.

9. If you don't have a _____ understanding of how your credit or debit card works, you might end up paying late fees or overdraft fees.

Add the ending -ic to change each word to an adjective.

10. a person who is very kind and good: angel _____

11. a beautiful view: scene _____

12. people who love their country: patriot _____

Review the Vocabulary

Circle the letter of the answer that best completes each sentence.

1. _____ would best help you **evaluate** yourself as a student.
   a. Your test scores
   b. Your friends
   c. Your books

2. To describe your **values**, you would explain _____.
   a. why you take the bus
   b. how much your new shoes costs
   c. who you ask for advice

3. One of the **consequences** of catching a cold is _____.
   a. spending time outside
   b. missing school or work
   c. making a bad decision

4. Setting a time **limit** will help you _____ online.
   a. start earlier
   b. get your phone
   c. spend less time

Complete each sentence with a word from the box.

adjust	appropriate	borrow	consequences	evaluate
limit	loan	specific	transfer	values

5. Jonathan needed money to buy a truck, so he went to the bank for a _____.

6. Before he got his own truck, he often had to _____ his brother's truck.

7. _____ use of a credit card can make your life a lot easier.

8. Marie spent a lot of time at the bank, or to be more _____, two and a half hours.

9. If you charge too much on your credit card, you may need to _____ your spending.

10. Danny had to _____ money to his checking account to pay his credit card bill.

Write two new sentences. Use a word from the box in each sentence.

11. _____

_____

12. _____

_____

Write a Narrative Paragraph

A narrative paragraph tells what happened during a period of time. Some narratives, like stories and novels, tell about made-up events. Other narratives can tell about real events, like a time when you had to make an important decision.

A narrative paragraph about a decision you had to make should include:

- ✔ The decision you had to make
- ✔ Why you had to make the decision
- ✔ How you made the decision
- ✔ A concluding sentence that wraps up your story

Read the prompt.

> In this lesson, you have read about how to make decisions. You have seen that it isn't always clear what decision to make. Write a paragraph about an important personal decision you have had to make. What were the consequences, either good or bad? What would you do differently now that you have learned how to make good decisions?

Plan Your Writing

Use the graphic organizer to think about your topic and take notes about what you will write.

What decision did you have to make?

Why did you have to make the decision?

How did you make the decision?

What happened as a result of making the decision?

Write Your Paragraph

On the lines below or on a computer, write a narrative paragraph about a decision you had to make.

_____

_____

_____

_____

_____

_____

_____

_____

_____

Review Your Writing

Use this list to check your writing.

- ☐ I told about a time I had to make an important decision.
- ☐ I explained why I had to make the decision.
- ☐ I described what I did.
- ☐ I wrote a concluding sentence.
- ☐ I checked punctuation and spelling

For practice with Frequently Confused Words, complete the Language Skills Mini-Lesson on page 136.

After you check your work, make any corrections. Read your paragraph aloud to a partner. Then discuss how your paragraphs were the same or different.

Think and Discuss

Imagine that you found out a friend or family member was doing something you think is wrong. Work in small groups to talk about the decision you have to make, the options you have, and possible consequences for each.

iStock.com / Fertnig

What would you do if you saw someone stealing money?

Read the article. Circle the best answer to each question.

Working the Night Shift

Construction crews often work at night.

1 Would you work the night shift? A night shift might go from 10 p.m. to 6 a.m. That's when most people are asleep. Nearly 15 million Americans work a night shift. Night shift work is common for some who work public service jobs like police, firefighters, and nurses. But some businesses also need night shift workers. For example, truck drivers, store and hotel clerks, and factory workers may all work nights.

2 Working the night shift can cause problems for some people. The biggest danger is to workers' health. Our bodies have a natural sleep cycle, so it can be hard for workers to sleep during the day. Lack of sleep can increase the risk of health problems, including heart disease, cancer, and obesity. Being sleepy also makes people more likely to have accidents. In addition to its effects on health, night shift work can make it hard to spend time with family and friends.

3 Working a night shift can have some benefits. Perhaps the biggest benefit is pay. Most jobs pay more for night shift work. A night work schedule can also give workers more time to do things. For example, they don't face as much traffic getting to and from work. They can attend classes, go to the doctor, or do errands during the day without missing work. At some jobs, workers can get more done at night. There are fewer meetings and distractions.

4 Not everyone can choose whether to work the day or night shift. But if you can choose, think about the possible risks and rewards.

1. Which sentence supports the idea that working the night shift has benefits?
   a. Not everyone can choose the shift they work.
   b. The human body has a natural sleep cycle.
   c. Night shifts usually go from around 10 p.m. to 6 a.m.
   d. Workers can earn more on a night shift.

2. How can a night shift help a worker's schedule?
   a. It gives them more time to go to appointments in the daytime.
   b. It helps them get more hours of sleep each day.
   c. It lets them attend more meetings at work.
   d. It gives them less time to spend with friends and family.

3. Why can working the night shift be harmful?
   a. Workers don't get paid enough.
   b. Workers have difficulty getting enough sleep.
   c. Workers spend a lot of time getting to work.
   d. Workers can't spend as much time with coworkers.

4. Which of these is an example of a public service job in the article?
   a. factory worker
   b. hotel clerk
   c. firefighter
   d. trucker

UNIT 2
Social Studies

Westward Expansion

In this lesson, you will

READ

two articles about how transportation helped the United States expand westward:

- The Oregon Trail
- The Transcontinental Railroad

USE THIS READING SKILL

Find the main idea and details

USE THIS VOCABULARY SKILL

Understand words with the roots *vers* and *vert*

USE THIS WRITING SKILL

Write an informative text

USE THESE KEY VOCABULARY WORDS

challenge a difficulty or a problem

combine to join two or more things together

convert to change someone's beliefs

doubt to be uncertain or not believe something

establish to set up or create something

exhausting causing you to feel very tired

former having to do with the past

progress movement forward; the process of getting closer to a goal

pursue to try to do something over a period of time

section a part of a whole

UNDERSTAND THESE CONTENT VOCABULARY WORDS

dynamite an explosive used to blast through rock

invasion the act of entering a place when you are not welcome

missionary a person who travels far from home to do religious work

terrain land of a certain type

transcontinental crossing the continent

Wagons travel west on the Oregon Trail.

Image courtesy of the National Park Service

Use the Vocabulary

Answer these questions about the vocabulary words. Use the definitions on page 40 to help you.

1. How can you make **progress** toward your education goals?

   _____

2. What kinds of activities do you find **exhausting**?

   _____

3. Describe some **challenges** you have faced. What was **challenging** about them?

   _____

4. What kind of career do you want to **pursue**? How will you **pursue** it?

   _____

5. Do you think the U.S. should try to **establish** a settlement on another planet? Why or why not?

   _____

6. Why might countries **combine** troops to fight an enemy?

   _____

7. What **section** of the grocery store has your favorite foods in it?

   _____

8. Would you be willing to **convert** to a different kind of diet from what you eat now? Why or why not?

   _____

9. What do you know about the **former** president of the United States?

   _____

10. Describe a time when you have **doubted** something you heard on the news. Why did you **doubt** it?

    _____

VOCABULARY TIP

When you read a word you don't know, look for clues in nearby text. You may see a synonym, or a word with similar meaning, that can help you understand the unknown word.

Read the sentences. Look for clues about the meaning of *exhausting*. Answer the question.

Tammy's job at the daycare center is **exhausting**. *She has to stay alert at all times. She also has to be very patient. She can't get frustrated when children don't listen. By the end of the day, she is very tired.*

Which word means about the same as *exhausting*?

   a. alert   c. frustrating

   b. patient   d. tiring

Preview

Before you read, preview the article. Read the title, the first paragraph, and the headings. Look at the map. Use the information to think about what you will learn.

1. What will this article be about? _____

2. What are the three headings? _____

3. What does the map show? _____

Visualize

As you read, visualize the details in the passage. When you visualize, you create a picture in your mind. This can help you understand and remember what you read.

Read the article. Visualize what happened. Answer the questions in the margin.

The Oregon Trail

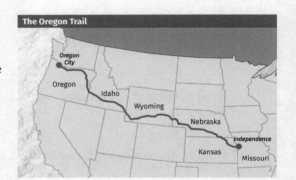

The Oregon Trail

1   The Oregon Trail was a 2,000-mile route from Independence, Missouri, to Oregon City, Oregon. In the mid-1800s, about 350,000 pioneers and emigrants used the Oregon Trail to **pursue** a better life in the west.

2   A variety of people traveled the Oregon Trail for different reasons. For years, Indians and fur trappers had used parts of it for hunting and trade. Later, missionaries used the trail to look for Indians they could **convert** to Christianity. Others who used the trail included farmers looking for free land in Oregon and miners heading to California to find gold.

Preparation

3   The trip on the Oregon Trail was expensive. Travelers needed approximately $1,000 to supply their trip. Settlers had to purchase a wagon and mules or oxen to pull it. They needed enough food and supplies to last the trip and to get settled after the journey. They had to pack cooking utensils, guns, tools and anything else they would need.

Life on the Trail

4   Each day on the trail, oxen had to be hitched and unhitched from wagons. Travelers needed to gather firewood and find fresh water. Wagons needed to be repaired. Meals had to be cooked over open fires. Settlers had to unpack and repack wagons every day as they set up camp. All this work was **exhausting**.

5   There were other difficulties on the trip. Wagons had to cross dangerous rivers and mountains. Long **sections** of the trail had no trees or shade in the hot sun. Dust covered everything and made breathing difficult. The trip took several months to complete, and the trail could be boring. Wagon trains might travel 12 hours a day but go only 15 miles.

6   Diseases and injuries were other problems faced by pioneers. People who were sick or hurt had little help on the trail. They had to walk or ride in a bumpy wagon. Around 20,000 emigrants died on the journey.

The End of the Trail

7   Between 1843 and 1869, the trail was improved. Towns **established** along the trail provided supplies. Ferries made it easier to cross rivers. Despite these improvements, few pioneers used the trail after 1869. That's when the new Transcontinental Railroad began providing a faster, easier, and cheaper way to travel west.

TIP
You *emigrate* **from** a place. You *immigrate* **to** a place.

What would it be like to get ready for this trip?

TIP
The trip would cost about $32,000 today.

What do you picture about making this trip?

Picture how the journey changed by 1869.

Check Your Comprehension

Answer these questions about the article.

1. Where did the Oregon Trail start and end? _____

2. Why was the trip difficult? _____

3. Look at the map. What do you notice about the route of the Oregon Trail? _____

_____

Find the Main Idea and Details

The main idea of a paragraph tells what the paragraph is mostly about. Sometimes the main idea is stated directly in one sentence. An author of informational text includes supporting details to describe or explain the main idea.

Reread paragraph 2. Underline the sentence that tells the main idea. Then write four details that support it.

> A variety of people traveled the Oregon Trail for different reasons. For years, Indians and fur trappers had used parts of it for hunting and trade. Later, missionaries used the trail to look for Indians they could **convert** to Christianity. Others who used the trail included farmers looking for free land in Oregon and miners heading to California to find gold.

1. _____

2. _____

3. _____

4. _____

A sentence telling the main idea can be anywhere in a paragraph. You will need to read a paragraph and think about which sentences give details or reasons before figuring out the main idea.

Reread paragraph 4. Underline the main idea. Then write four details that tell more about the main idea.

> Each day on the trail, oxen had to be hitched and unhitched from wagons. Travelers needed to gather firewood and find fresh water. Wagons needed to be repaired. Meals had to be cooked over open fires. Settlers had to unpack and repack wagons every day as they set up camp. All this work was **exhausting**.

5. _____

6. _____

7. _____

8. _____

 IMPROVE YOUR READING

Practice reading paragraph 5 of "The Oregon Trail" silently. Sound out any words you do not know. After you have practiced reading the paragraph, read it aloud to a partner. Pay attention to your speed.

Practice the Skills

Preview the article. Answer the questions.

1. Read the title. What is this article about? _____

2. What parts is the article organized into? _____

3. Look at the map. What does it show? _____

Read the article. As you read, visualize what happened. Answer the questions in the margin.

The Transcontinental Railroad

1 Before the 1860s, a trip across the North American continent was long, dangerous, and expensive. The Transcontinental Railroad lowered travel costs from $1,000 to $150 and reduced travel time from six months to a week. The railroad forever changed the country. Shipping goods across the country and settling new lands became easy.

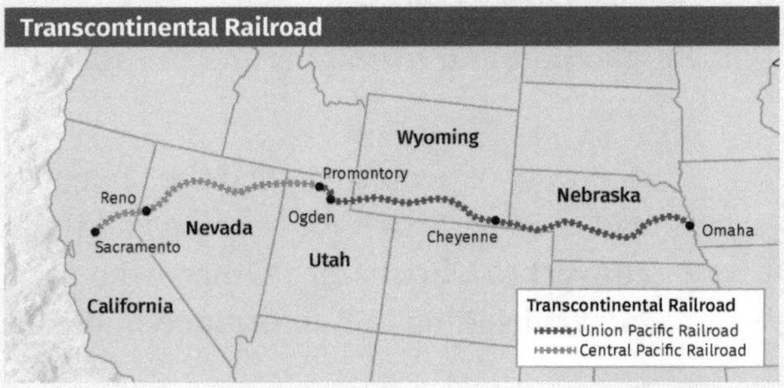

Transcontinental Railroad

(map showing: Reno, Sacramento, Nevada, California, Promontory, Ogden, Utah, Wyoming, Cheyenne, Nebraska, Omaha. Legend: Transcontinental Railroad — Union Pacific Railroad, Central Pacific Railroad)

2 Two companies, the Union Pacific Railroad and the Central Pacific Railroad, competed with each other to build the railroad. They raced to lay track from opposite directions until they met in the middle.

What do you picture about how the railroad companies worked?

The Union Pacific Railroad

3 The Union Pacific Railroad started construction in Omaha, Nebraska, and worked from east to west. The company had two advantages. First, it got to start on flat land, so workers made quick **progress** in the beginning. Second, it had a ready supply of workers because **former** Civil War soldiers needed jobs.

4 However, the railroad workers did face some **challenges**. The building of the railroad forced some Native Americans off their lands. The Sioux, Arapaho, and Cheyenne Indians referred to the railroad as the "iron horse." They saw it as a threat to their way of life and an invasion of their lands. They attacked railroad workers. They tore up newly laid track. Some stole equipment, supplies, and livestock.

The Central Pacific Railroad

What do you picture about working in the mountains?

5 The Central Pacific Railroad started in Sacramento, California, and worked east. It faced different challenges. It had to cross difficult mountain terrain. In the Sierra Nevada mountains, workers used dynamite to blast tunnels through rock, and made as little as 1 to 2 feet of progress per day. Extreme cold and huge snowstorms made work difficult. But the biggest problem was a lack of labor.

What do the details about Chinese workers help you understand?

6 The railroad hired Chinese immigrants. Many people **doubted** the Chinese could do the work. But eventually, 80 percent of the workforce was Chinese. These workers often worked 12-hour days in harsh conditions. They were given the most dangerous jobs like blasting and handling dynamite. They were paid less than white workers. And they were sometimes whipped by their white managers. Around 1,200 Chinese workers died building the railroad.

7 The tracks laid by the Union Pacific and the Central Pacific finally met in Promontory Summit, Utah, on May 10, 1869. The two companies had **combined** to lay more than 1,700 miles of track that connected two parts of the country.

Chinese railroad workers

Check Your Comprehension

Answer these questions about the article.

1. How did the railroad change the trip from the east to the west? _____

2. What two companies built the railroad? _____

3. What can you tell from the map? _____

Practice Finding the Main Idea and Details

The main idea is the point the author wants to make. Supporting details are reasons and examples that support the main idea. In some paragraphs, the main idea is stated in a single sentence. In other paragraphs, the main idea is implied. If the main idea is implied, you must read all the sentences and figure out how they are related.

Reread paragraph 4. Write the main idea and supporting details in the boxes.

STATED MAIN IDEA
1.

DETAIL	DETAIL	DETAIL	DETAIL
2.	3.	4.	5.

HINT
Look at the details first to figure out how they are related.

Reread paragraph 6. Write the implied main idea and supporting details in the boxes.

IMPLIED MAIN IDEA
6.

DETAIL	DETAIL	DETAIL	DETAIL
7.	8.	9.	10.

IMPROVE YOUR READING

Listen and read along while your teacher reads paragraph 1 of "The Transcontinental Railroad" aloud. Then read the paragraph aloud with your teacher. Pay attention to your expression.

DEVELOP YOUR UNDERSTANDING

Respond to the Readings

Answer these questions about the articles.

1. Why was it expensive to travel on the Oregon Trail? _____

    _____

2. What are some reasons so many people might have died during the trip west on the Oregon Trail?

    _____

3. What is the main idea of the article "The Oregon Trail"?

    a. Around 350,000 people faced difficult conditions on the Oregon Trail to reach the west.

    b. The Oregon Trail went from Independence, Missouri, to Oregon City, Oregon, and crossed mountains and rivers.

    c. Towns established along the Oregon Trail and ferries that crossed rivers made it easier to move west.

    > **HINT**
    > The main idea tells what the whole article is about.

4. Why was building a railroad harder in the mountains than on the flat prairies? _____

    _____

5. What is the main idea of "The Transcontinental Railroad"? _____

    _____

6. How did both the Oregon Trail and the Transcontinental Railroad speed up settlement of the west?

    _____

Use Word Parts: Roots *vers* and *vert*

To figure out the meaning of a word, you can look for a word root that you know. A root is a word part that can be joined to prefixes and suffixes to form words. The roots *vers* and *vert* mean "turn." For example, the word *convert* can mean "to turn or change your beliefs."

Read each sentence. Use context clues, your knowledge of word parts, or a dictionary to write the meaning of the underlined word.

> **TIP**
> The root *ver* is similar to *vers* and *vert* but has a different meaning. The root *ver* means "*truth*." It's found in words like *verify* and *verdict*.

1. Molly is an <u>introvert</u>. She prefers to stay home rather than go out with a lot of people.

    _____

2. Bella is an <u>extrovert</u>. She is a social person who loves parties and going out with friends.

    _____

3. The decision to cancel the TV show was very unpopular, so the TV network <u>reversed</u> its decision.

    _____

4. Before workers could build a dam on the river, they had to <u>divert</u> the water.

    _____

5. To get ketchup out of the bottle, you may need to <u>invert</u> the bottle.

    _____

Review the Vocabulary

Circle the letter of the answer that best completes each sentence.

1. If someone is your **former** boss, then _____.
   a. they are your favorite boss
   b. you worked for them before
   c. they treated you unfairly

2. If something is a **challenge**, that means that _____.
   a. it is expensive
   b. it is fun
   c. it is difficult

3. If you **combine** two things, you _____.
   a. compare them to each other
   b. bring them home
   c. put them together

4. If you did something **exhausting**, you would probably _____.
   a. want to take a nap
   b. go out and run a race
   c. look for a new place to live

Complete each sentence with a word from the box.

challenge	combine	converted	doubted	establish
exhausting	former	progress	pursued	section

5. Andy _____ his dream and became a teacher last year.

6. Becky works as a volunteer and cleans the _____ of the hiking trail that is along the lake.

7. Bill is making _____ cleaning his desk. He sorts a few papers each day.

8. There were only five minutes left in class, so I _____ that I could write an essay in that time.

9. The governor used to be a Democrat, but he _____ to Republican 20 years ago.

10. The car company wants to _____ offices and a factory in the United States.

Write two new sentences. Use a word from the box in each sentence.

11. _____

_____

12. _____

_____

Write an Informative Text

Informative texts give facts about a topic. They may give definitions, examples, and details that tell you more about the topic. They do not give the author's opinion or feelings about a topic or try to persuade readers to do something. Some common examples of informative texts are news articles, business reports, and textbooks.

An informative text should include:

- ✔ A sentence that tells your topic and main idea
- ✔ Details and information about a topic, including facts, definitions, and examples
- ✔ Organization that groups related information in paragraphs
- ✔ Words and phrases that connect your ideas, such as *for example, also, because, another*
- ✔ A conclusion that relates to your main idea

Read the prompt.

> Write an informative text about what it was like to travel on the Oregon Trail. Include details and information from the article "The Oregon Trail" and from your own research. Organize your ideas.

Plan Your Writing

Before you begin writing, review the article again. Take notes about details you want to include. Research the Oregon Trail online or in books. Then use the graphic organizer to plan your informative text.

TIP
Each paragraph should have a main idea.

Topic/ Main Idea: _____   _____
Detail 1: _____   _____   Detail 2: _____   _____   Detail 3: _____   _____   Detail 4: _____   _____
Conclusion: _____   _____

Write Your Informative Text

On the lines below or on a computer, write an informative text about traveling on the Oregon Trail.

_____

_____

_____

_____

_____

_____

_____

_____

Review Your Writing

Use this list to check your writing.

- [ ] I stated my topic and main idea.
- [ ] I included details and information.
- [ ] I used words that connect ideas.
- [ ] I wrote a concluding sentence.
- [ ] I used capital letters correctly.

For practice with capitalization, complete the Writing Skills Mini-Lesson on page 137.

After you check your work, make any corrections. Read your informative text aloud to a partner. Then discuss the information you each included in your text.

Think and Discuss

Many emigrants kept diaries or journals on the Oregon Trail. Read these excerpts from two travelers:

"The road today was very hilly and rough. At night we encamped within one mile of Fort Hall. Mosquitoes were as thick as flakes in a snow storm. The poor horses whinnied all night, from their bites."

—Margaret A. Frink, July 11, 1850

"Raining all day ... and the boys are all soaking wet and look sad and comfortless. The little ones and myself are shut up in the wagons from the rain. Still it will find its way in and many things are wet; and take us all together we are a poor looking set, and all this for Oregon . . . I am thinking as I write, 'Oh Oregon, you must be a wonderful country.'"

—Amelia Stewart Knight, June 1, 1853

Talk about each excerpt in small groups. What do the excerpts help you understand about the trip? Why might people have wanted to write their experiences in journals?

Voting Rights

In this lesson, you will

READ

multiple texts about voting rights:
- Texts about the Fifteenth Amendment
- Texts about Women's Suffrage

USE THIS READING SKILL

Analyze purpose and point of view

USE THIS VOCABULARY SKILL

Understand words with the prefix *inter-*

USE THIS WRITING SKILL

Write a letter to the editor

Women march in 1912 for the right to vote.

USE THESE KEY VOCABULARY WORDS

allow to let something happen or be done

barrier something that blocks movement or gets in the way of action

competition the act of trying to get or win something

consistent always acting the same way or having a regular pattern

cooperation the act of working together to get something done

deny to refuse to give a person something they ask for

eligible able to do something or be chosen for something

emphasize to give special attention to something

influence to affect or change what someone does

interpret to understand the meaning of something

UNDERSTAND THESE CONTENT VOCABULARY WORDS

ballot a piece of paper used to vote in an election

legislation a law or set of laws passed by the government

literacy the ability to read and write

register to put your name on an official list

suffrage the right to vote in government elections

Use the Vocabulary

Answer these questions about the vocabulary words. Use the definitions on page 50 to help you.

1. What are some **barriers** to getting a college degree?

   _____

2. What are two examples of **cooperation** in the workplace?

   _____

3. At what age do you think people should be **eligible** to get a driver's license? Why?

   _____

4. How would you feel if a bank **denied** you a loan or a credit card? Explain.

   _____

5. Are you **allowed** to use a cell phone during a test? Explain.

   _____

6. Think of a skill you have. If you were teaching someone that skill, what would you **emphasize**? Why?

   _____

7. Describe what you do when you **interpret** a reading passage or article.

   _____

8. Do you think **competition** between students in a class is a good or bad thing? Explain.

   _____

9. How does the weather **influence** what you wear?

   _____

10. Why is it important for a cook in a restaurant to be **consistent** in how he makes food?

    _____

VOCABULARY TIP

When you read a word you don't know, look for clues in the surrounding sentences. Sometimes authors will give examples that help you figure out a word's meaning.

Look for examples of *barriers* in the sentences below. Answer the questions.

*There can be many **barriers** to buying your first home. For example, many people don't understand the process. Others have not saved enough money. Another problem is a low credit score that stops people from getting a loan.*

1. What are the examples of *barriers*? _____

2. What is the definition of *barriers* in your own words? _____

Skim

Before you closely read each text, skim it to find out what it will be about. Read the description of each text. Read a few sentences. Look at what the text in the box is about.

1. What is Text 1 about? _____

2. What is Text 2 about? _____

3. What does the text in the graphic box tell about? _____

Take Notes

When you read a text, take notes about the most important information and details.

Read the texts. Pay attention to important information. Make notes in the margin.

The Fifteenth Amendment

Text 1: An article about voting rights for African Americans

Underline what Text 1 is about.

1   After the Civil War, African Americans were freed from slavery. However, many black men were still not **allowed** to vote. As a result, Congress passed the Fifteenth Amendment to the U.S. Constitution in 1870. It states: "The right of citizens of the United States to vote shall not be **denied** . . . on account of race, color, or previous condition of servitude."

Make a note about what a poll tax was.

2   However, southern states made voting nearly impossible for African Americans in the 1890s. States created poll taxes, annual fees that had to be paid to vote. Many African Americans simply couldn't afford to pay.

Rules for the State of Mississippi
+ **MUST** LIVE IN THE STATE TWO YEARS.
+ **MUST** HAVE PAID ALL TAXES BY FEBRUARY 1.
+ **MUST** PAY AN ANNUAL POLL TAX OF TWO DOLLARS TO THE STATE, AND UP TO ONE DOLLAR TO THE COUNTY.
+ **MUST** BE REGISTERED, AND IN ORDER TO DO SO MUST BE ABLE TO READ ANY SECTION OF THE STATE CONSTITUTION AND GIVE A REASONABLE INTERPRETATION OF IT.
+ **ANY PERSON CONVICTED OF A SERIOUS CRIME IS FOREVER BARRED FROM VOTING.**

Underline the part that tells what literacy tests were.

3   Literacy tests were another **barrier**. In Mississippi, people who applied to vote had to read and **interpret** parts of the state constitution. Many ex-slaves could not read at all. Those who could were given difficult passages. White officials decided who passed and who failed.

4   The rules kept black men from voting, and by 1892, fewer than 6% were registered to vote in Mississippi.

Text 2: Adapted from "What a Colored Man Should Do to Vote," an early 1900s pamphlet

Make a note about when men should vote.

1   You cannot value too highly your right to vote, which is your choice of who will control your interests.

2   You should vote at every election. In national and congressional elections, vote for the best interests of the country. In local elections, vote for the best interests of your community. Never sell your vote.

Underline some of the general advice the author gives.

3   *General Advice:* You are urged to pay all your taxes on time, especially your poll tax.

4   Avoid committing any crime, great or small, as it can take away your right to vote and cause you lasting shame.

5   As voters, you should seek to be friendly with your white neighbors, so that you may consult with them about your common interests. It cannot be **emphasized** too strongly, that nothing should **influence** your vote except a desire to serve the best interests of the country and your state.

Check Your Comprehension

Answer these questions about the two texts.

1. What did the Fifteenth Amendment do? _____

2. What was a poll tax? _____

3. What information can you get from Text 2? _____

Analyze Purpose and Point of View

An author's purpose is the reason he or she writes about a topic. Some common purposes for writing are to inform, explain, persuade, and entertain. Sometimes a text will have more than one purpose. An author's point of view is how the author sees events or information. To figure out an author's point of view, think about what the author wants you to understand about the topic.

Answer the questions about the texts.

1. Reread paragraph 1 of Text 1. What does this paragraph tell about?
   a. how the author feels about the Civil War
   b. what the Fifteenth Amendment did

2. In Text 1, what are two examples of how southern states made voting difficult for African American men?

   _____

3. In paragraph 4 of Text 1, what evidence is used to show that the rules prevented black men from voting?

   _____

4. What is the main purpose of Text 1?
   a. to inform
   b. to persuade
   c. to entertain

5. Reread the first sentence of Text 2. Does it describe a fact or an opinion? _____

6. Should African American men vote, according to the author of Text 2? _____

7. What does the section "General Advice" in Text 2 tell about? _____

8. Which sentence describes the point of view of the author of Text 2?
   a. He thinks African American men are treated unfairly.
   b. He thinks it is very important for African American men to vote.
   c. He thinks that Mississippi has a lot of rules for voters to follow.

   HINT
   Phrases such as *you should*, *you are urged*, *you are warned* tell the reader what to do.

9. Is the main purpose of Text 2 to inform people or to persuade them to vote? _____

 IMPROVE YOUR READING

Listen and read along silently as your teacher reads paragraph 2 of Text 2. Pay attention to your teacher's tone and expression. Then read the paragraph aloud with your teacher.

Practice the Skills

Skim Text 3 and Text 4. Then answer the questions.

1. What is Text 3 about? _____

2. What is Text 4 about? _____

3. What do the poster and postcard show? _____

Read the texts. As you read, make notes in the margin about important ideas.

Women's Suffrage

Text 3: Adapted from a 1918 flyer by the National American Woman Suffrage Association

DO IT NOW!
GIVE THE VOTE TO THE WOMEN OF EVERY STATE BY
Federal Constitutional Amendment.

BECAUSE—Woman suffrage is happening all the world around; few deny it—why should the United States delay?

BECAUSE—Great Britain and Canada gave women voting rights within a year. The women of Finland, Norway, Denmark, Iceland, Australia and New Zealand had suffrage on equal terms with men before our country entered [World War I]. What other countries have done in war time, our country can do.

BECAUSE—The government that asks women to give their all to win a war for democracy in Europe cannot **consistently** deny them the vote, the symbol of democracy, at home.

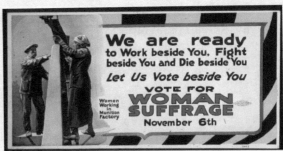

A woman and a man at work in a weapons factory

BECAUSE—The woman suffrage movement is a part of the great struggle for human freedom, and until the amendment is passed, the fight for suffrage must and will go on.

SUPPORT THE FEDERAL SUFFRAGE AMENDMENT

Text 4: Excerpts from "Household Hints," a pamphlet by the National Association Opposed to Woman Suffrage

Votes of women can accomplish no more than votes of men. Why waste time, energy, and money without result?

Housewives!

- You do not need a ballot to clean out your sink spout.
- Control of the temper makes a happier home than control of elections.
- Why vote for pure food laws, when your husband does that, while you can purify your ice-box?
- Clean houses and good homes, which cannot be provided by legislation, keep children healthier and happier than any number of uplift laws.

Vote NO on Woman Suffrage

BECAUSE 90% of the women either do not want it, or do not care.

BECAUSE it means **competition** of women with men instead of **cooperation**.

BECAUSE 80% of the women **eligible** to vote are married and can only double or cancel out their husbands' votes.

BECAUSE in some states more voting women than voting men will place the government under petticoat rule.

BECAUSE it is unwise to risk the good we already have for the evil which may occur.

An early 1900s political postcard against suffrage.

Check Your Comprehension

Answer these questions about the article.

1. What does the author of Text 3 want readers to do?

   _____

HINT

Look at the first and last lines of the flyer.

2. What does the author of Text 4 think about voting rights for women?

   _____

3. What is the message of the "We are ready" poster? _____

Practice Analyzing Purpose and Point of View

An author's purpose is the reason he or she writes about a topic. An author's point of view is what the author thinks about a topic.

An author of informational text states facts and usually has a neutral point of view about the topic. An author of persuasive text may have a positive or negative view of a topic or issue. To determine point of view, think about how the author presents information and what words the author chooses.

Complete the graphic organizer with information from the selections.

	TEXT 3	TEXT 4	POSTCARD
Type of Text	A flyer from the National American Woman Suffrage Association	A pamphlet by the National Association Opposed to Woman Suffrage	A political postcard against Woman Suffrage
How is the information presented and organized?	1.	4.	7.
What does the author want the reader to understand? **How does the author support his or her ideas?**	2.	5.	8.
What is the author's point of view on the topic of women's voting?	3.	6.	9.

 Fluency **IMPROVE YOUR READING**

Practice reading paragraphs 1 through 3 of Text 3. As you read, pay attention to punctuation marks. After you have read the text two or three times, read it aloud to a partner.

Respond to the Readings

Answer these questions about the articles.

1. Based on information from Text 1, how could literacy tests be used unfairly to stop African Americans from voting?

_____

2. Reread the voting rules for the state of Mississippi from Text 1. How do you know it was hard to meet all these rules? Use what you learned from Text 1.

_____

3. How are Text 3 and the poster similar?

_____

4. Compare how the authors of Text 3 and Text 4 view women's right to vote.

_____

_____

HINT
Think about the information about African American voting rights in Texts 1 and 2. Think about the views against women's suffrage in Text 4 and the postcard.

5. What have you learned about the history of voting rights based on the texts in this lesson? Based on what you learned, has it been easy for people to get or use their right to vote?

_____

_____

Use Word Parts: Prefix *inter-*

The prefix *inter-* means "between" or "among." One meaning of the word *interpret*, for example, is "to translate words between languages."

Match each word from the box with its definition below. Use a dictionary if you don't know the meaning of a word.

TIP
The prefix *inter-* is sometimes added to words that stand alone, as in *interstate*. Other times, it is added to a word root, as in *intercept*.

interact	interfere	intermission	international
internet	interpreter	interrupt	interstate

1. _____ between nations

2. _____ a system that connects computers throughout the world

3. _____ to say something while someone else is speaking

4. _____ to do things with one another

5. _____ a person who translates between languages

6. _____ to get involved between others when your help is not wanted

7. _____ between states

8. _____ the break between parts of a play or concert

Review the Vocabulary

Read each group of words. Write the vocabulary word from the box that best goes with each group of words.

allow	barrier	competition	consistent	cooperation
denied	eligible	emphasize	influence	interpret

1. partnership, aid, teamwork _____

2. to approve, to permit, to let happen _____

3. to stress, to point out, to underline _____

4. obstacle, difficulty, restriction _____

5. same, constant, regular _____

Complete each sentence with a word from the box.

6. The teacher asked the class to read a poem and _____ the its meaning.

7. The bank _____ Paul's application for a loan because he has too much credit card debt.

8. The car salesperson used information about gas mileage to _____ my decision to buy the car.

9. A spelling bee is a kind of _____ in which people try to spell the most words correctly.

10. To be _____ to run for president of the United States, a person must be at least 35 years old.

Write two new sentences. Use a word from the box in each sentence.

11. _____

_____

12. _____

_____

Write a Letter to the Editor

In this lesson, you read excerpts from a flyer and a pamphlet that were persuasive texts. Both the flyer and the pamphlet urged readers to take action on the issue of women's suffrage. The writers chose words to help persuade their audience. They each gave reasons to support their ideas.

A letter to the editor of a newspaper can also be a persuasive text. It can provide information and encourage readers to take action on an issue.

A letter to the editor should include:

- ✔ A statement of what action you want the reader to take
- ✔ Reasons that support your point of view
- ✔ Words that persuade and link your reasons and opinions
- ✔ A concluding sentence that wraps up the ideas in your letter

Read the prompt.

> Write a letter to the editor of a newspaper to convince readers that they should vote. Provide reasons that support your ideas. Include information about how people can register to vote in your area.

Plan Your Writing

Before you begin writing, think about your purpose and your audience. Your purpose is to persuade people to vote and to tell them how they can register to vote. Research some of the reasons that will convince your audience. Use the graphic organizer to plan your letter to the editor.

TIP
Address your letter to the editor. Include a closing with your name.

| My Opinion: _____ |
| _____ |

| Reason #1: _____ |
| _____ |

| Reason #2: _____ |
| _____ |

| Reason #3: _____ |
| _____ |

| Conclusion: _____ |
| _____ |

Write Your Letter to the Editor

On the lines below or on a computer, write your letter to the editor.

_____

_____

_____

_____

_____

_____

_____

Review Your Writing

Use this list to check your writing.

- ☐ I stated my point of view.
- ☐ I gave reasons to support my view.
- ☐ I used words to persuade and link ideas.
- ☐ I wrote a concluding sentence.
- ☐ I checked capitalization and spelling.

After you check your work, make any corrections. Read your letter aloud to a partner. Listen to your partner's letter. Compare how your letters are similar and different.

Think and Discuss

Former slave Frederick Douglass worked to end slavery and to get voting rights for both African American men and for women. In an 1869 speech at a women's rights convention, Douglass discussed why he felt that black men needed voting rights first:

"I do not see how anyone can pretend that there is the same urgency in giving the ballot to woman as to the Negro. With us, the matter is a question of life and death, at least, in fifteen States of the Union. When women, because they are women, are hunted down through the cities of New York and New Orleans; . . . when their children are torn from their arms; . . . when they are in danger of having their homes burnt down over their heads; when their children are not allowed to enter schools; then they will have an urgency to obtain the ballot equal to our own."

—Frederick Douglass, 1869

Frederick Douglass

In small groups, discuss what Frederick Douglass' argument is. How does he describe what life is like for African Americans? Do you think he makes a good point?

World War II

In this lesson, you will

READ

two articles about World War II:
- The Home Front
- Navajo Code Talkers

USE THIS READING SKILL

Make inferences

USE THIS VOCABULARY SKILL

Understand words with the suffix *-ive*

USE THIS WRITING SKILL

Write a narrative paragraph

A poster encouraging people to grow food during World War II

USE THESE KEY VOCABULARY WORDS

code a set of words, letters, symbols, or numbers used to secretly send messages to someone

critical very important

distribute to deliver

effort everything that is being done to achieve a goal

encourage to make someone more confident or more likely to do something

extensive very full or complete

fluent able to speak a language easily and very well

represent to be a sign or symbol of something

sacrifice the act of giving up something to gain something you consider more important

weapons things such as guns or knives that are used for fighting

UNDERSTAND THESE CONTENT VOCABULARY WORDS

basic training the first few weeks of training when someone joins the military

home front the nonmilitary people of a country at war and their activities in support of the war effort

rationing when the government limits the amount people can have of something when there isn't a lot available

recruits new people in the armed forces

submarine a ship that can operate under water

tank a military vehicle that moves on two large metal belts with wheels inside

Use the Vocabulary

Answer these questions about the vocabulary words. Use the definitions on page 60 to help you.

1. What is something you've put a lot of **effort** into achieving?

   _____

2. Do you think people should be able to carry **weapons** freely? Explain your answer.

   _____

3. What are some advantages to being **fluent** in more than one language?

   _____

4. What is one of the most **critical** decisions you've ever made?

   _____

5. Name three things that **represent** the United States.

   _____

6. Who are the people who have **encouraged** you the most in life? What did they do?

   _____

7. What are two different jobs that require **extensive** training?

   _____

8. Name a job where people use **code** to communicate.

   _____

9. Name two everyday items that people **distribute**.

   _____

10. Tell about something you'd make **sacrifices** for.

    _____

    HINT
    The word *sacrifice* can be a noun or a verb.

VOCABULARY TIP

Some words have more than one meaning when you look them up in a dictionary. Look at these definitions for *critical*:

critical (adjective)

a. of the greatest importance   b. using careful judgment   c. saying that someone or something is bad or wrong

Write the letter of the definition that matches how critical is used in each sentence.

_____ 1. Charlie's boss was very *critical* of his work and pointed out several things he needs to improve.

_____ 2. I learned that you use your *critical* thinking skills whenever you read.

_____ 3. Our boss said it was *critical* to complete the project on time and on budget.

Set a Purpose for Reading

Before you start to read, it's important to establish a purpose. The purpose is what you want to accomplish by the end of the reading. Ask yourself, *Why am I reading?* and *What do I hope to learn?* When you read with a purpose, it's easier to stay focused.

1. Look at the title, the poster, and the caption. What will this article be about? _____

2. What do you already know about life during World War II? _____

3. What do you think you might learn from reading this article? _____

Ask and Answer Questions

We ask questions all of the time to help us gather information and learn new ideas. Good readers ask questions as they read to help them understand what they are reading. As you read, check that the article makes sense by stopping and asking yourself questions.

Read the article. Check that you understand what you are reading. Write questions in the margin as you read.

The Home Front

1 The United States entered World War II on December 8, 1941. The war **effort** quickly became part of everyday life on the home front. Everyone made **sacrifices**.

Food Rationing

Example: What foods were rationed?

2 Food rationing began in the spring of 1942 as a way to fairly **distribute** food that was in short supply. Americans were given ration books that contained removable stamps that they could use to get items like sugar, meat, cheese, butter, and canned food. The government decided the number of points needed for items based on what was available and what people wanted. Having a ration book, however, did not mean that the things that people wanted would be in the stores they went to. Wartime cookbooks were written with rationing in mind.

Victory Gardens

What question can you ask about victory gardens?

3 The U.S. government **encouraged** people to grow their own food in family and public gardens, known as "victory gardens." By 1945, there were more than 20 million victory gardens that produced at least 40 percent of all vegetables grown during the war.

Rubber, Gas, and Oil Rationing

What question can you ask about other kinds of rationing?

4 Fresh food was also limited due to fuel and tire rationing. It was more important to use those materials to transport soldiers and war supplies than to transport food. There were ration books for rubber, gas, and oil. Each book had rules and deadlines. Rationing of gas and tires, for example, was based on the distance from your home to your job. A nationwide speed limit of 35 miles per hour, called the "victory speed," was set to get Americans to drive slower to save gas and rubber. No new cars were made during the war.

5 People felt it was their patriotic duty to collect products made of rubber and metal as well as kitchen fat, newspapers, and rags. Children organized metal drives in their neighborhoods to collect old toys, pots and pans, and even bottle caps. All of these were used to build **weapons** and other items needed for the war effort.

There were competitions to see which town, county, and state collected the most scrap. This poster is from Pennsylvania.

Check Your Comprehension

Answer these questions about the article.

1. What foods were rationed? _____

2. What was a victory garden? _____

3. How did children help the war effort? _____

Make Inferences

Writers often do not explain everything to the reader, so sometimes you have to make an inference. An inference is a conclusion you make by connecting what you already know or have read with new information. You "read between the lines" or find small clues that lead you to infer, or understand, things that the author doesn't state directly.

Reread the paragraphs 2 and 4 below. Then write *I* next to the statements that can be inferred from the paragraphs and *X* next to the statements that cannot.

Food rationing began in the spring of 1942 as a way to fairly **distribute** food that was in short supply. Americans were given ration books that contained removable stamps that they could use to get items like sugar, meat, cheese, butter, and canned food. The government decided the number of points needed for items based on what was available and what people wanted. Having a ration book, however, did not mean that the things that people wanted would be in the stores they went to. Wartime cookbooks were written with rationing in mind.

_____ **1.** All food was in short supply during World War II.

_____ **2.** It was OK to use the stamps in a ration book at different times.

_____ **3.** A person could not buy a rationed item without also giving the grocer the right ration stamp.

_____ **4.** Rationed items were always available.

_____ **5.** The recipes in wartime cookbooks used very little sugar, meat, cheese, and butter.

Fresh food was also limited due to fuel and tire rationing. It was more important to use those materials to transport soldiers and war supplies than to transport food. There were ration books for rubber, gas, and oil. Each book had rules and deadlines. Rationing of gas and tires, for example, was based on the distance from your home to your job. A nationwide speed limit of 35 miles per hour, called the "victory speed," was set to get Americans to drive slower to save gas and rubber. No new cars were made during the war.

_____ **6.** The farther you lived from where you worked, the more gas you got.

_____ **7.** The speed limit was raised to 35 miles an hour during the war.

_____ **8.** People were encouraged to carpool or walk to school, to work, and to go shopping.

 IMPROVE YOUR READING

Work in pairs. Listen to your teacher read paragraph 4 of "The Home Front." Pay attention to punctuation and pauses Then read the paragraph aloud in your group, along with your teacher.

Practice the Skills

Set a purpose for reading. Think about what you're going to read and learn about.

1. Look at the title, the photo, and the caption. What will this article be about? _____

2. What does the photo tell you about the code talkers? _____

3. What do you think you might learn from reading this article? _____

Read the article. Monitor your understanding as you read. Write questions in the margin as you read.

TIP
Navajo is pronounced **nav**-*a*-*ho*.

What question do you have about why the Marines used Navajo as the basis for a code?

What question do you have about how the Navajo code was created?

What question do you have about what the code talkers did?

Navajo Code Talkers

1 During war, messages need to be delivered and received quickly and in **code**. During World War II, the Navajo code talkers of the U.S. Marine Corps developed one of the most successful codes ever used. It was never broken.

2 The idea to use Navajo came from Philip Johnston, who was not Navajo, but was **fluent** in the language. He believed that Navajo was a good choice because the language had no written form and was spoken by very few people who weren't Navajo.

3 In the spring of 1942, 29 Navajo recruits, along with Johnston and the Marine Corps, started to create a code based on their native language. Their

Navajo code talkers operate a radio during World War II.

code used a common Navajo word to **represent** every letter of the English alphabet. The more commonly used letters were represented by several words in order to make the code even more difficult to crack. They spelled words using the first letter of the English word that the Navajo word translated to. For example, the Navajo word *shush* stood for the letter *b* because it means *bear* in English.

4 The Navajo often had to make up new words or use old words in new ways. For example, the names of different birds were used for different kinds of planes. The code word for *tank* became *wakaree´e*, or *turtle*, after one recruit commented that a tank was like a turtle because it had a hard shell and it moves. They also used word combinations to create code. For example, because the Navajo had no word for *submarine*, they used *besh-lo*, meaning "iron fish."

5 Once the code was completed, the Marine Corps established a Navajo code talkers program to train new recruits. In addition to basic training, they learned the code and got **extensive** training in how to set up, operate, and maintain telephone and radio equipment. Approximately 400 Navajos became code talkers.

6 Code talkers served in every major battle in the Pacific from 1942 to 1945. They performed general Marine duties, but their most important job was to communicate **critical** information quickly and accurately. In doing so, they saved thousands of lives.

Check Your Comprehension

Answer these questions about the article.

1. Who was Philip Johnston? _____

2. What made the Navajo language a good choice to use to create a code? _____

3. What kind of equipment did the code talkers learn to use? _____

Practice Making Inferences

A graphic organizer can help you use what you read and what you already know to make inferences.

Read this example with a sentence from paragraph 3. Then make your own inference using a sentence from the article.

WHAT I READ	WHAT I ALREADY KNEW
The more commonly used letters were represented by several words in order to make the code even more difficult to crack.	The letter *e* is commonly used in English.

↓   ↓

MY INFERENCE
There were several words used to represent the letter *e*.

WHAT I READ	WHAT I ALREADY KNEW

↓   ↓

MY INFERENCE

 IMPROVE YOUR READING

Reread paragraph 5 of "Navajo Code Talkers" silently. As you read, pause at punctuation marks like commas and periods. Work with a partner. Take turns reading one sentence at a time.

Respond to the Readings

Answer these questions about the articles.

1. What was the war effort? _____

2. Why were fuel and rubber rationed during World War II? _____

_____

3. The author wrote that Navajo "was spoken by very few people who weren't Navajo." Why is that an important fact?

_____

4. What were some of the duties of a code talker? _____

_____

5. People on the home front made sacrifices. So did the code talkers. How were they the same and different?

_____

Use Word Parts: Suffix -*ive*

The suffix -*ive* means "tending toward" or "having the nature of." When -*ive* is added to the end of a word, root, or base, it creates an adjective. If a word ends in *e*, drop the *e* before adding -*ive*.

Add the suffix -*ive* to the nouns in the first column. Use a dictionary to check your spelling.

	+ -*ive*
1. act	
2. appreciate	
3. attract	
4. cooperate	

	+ -*ive*
5. create	
6. decide	
7. effect	
8. expense	

TIP
Drop the final *de* or *d* and add -*sive* to words like *extend* to form the adjective *extensive*.

Write an adjective that ends in -*ive* from the box to complete each sentence. Use a dictionary if you don't know the meaning of a word.

9. Navajo code talkers were very _____ in sending and receiving messages quickly and accurately.

10. Since meat was rationed during the war, women had to be _____ when cooking for their families.

11. Public victory gardens were shared by _____ neighbors.

12. People on the home front were encouraged to be _____ in the war effort by collecting paper, metal, and rags.

Write two sentences that use a word with the suffix -*ive*.

13. _____

14. _____

Review the Vocabulary

Read each group of words. Write the vocabulary word from the box that best goes with each group of words.

code	critical	distribute	effort	encourage
extensive	fluent	represent	sacrifices	weapons

1. essential, necessary, must-have _____

2. large, major, great _____

3. act as, stand for, equal _____

4. give away, share, hand out _____

5. gun, knife, rifle _____

Complete each sentence with a word from the box.

6. The Choctaw Indians were the first Native Americans to use their language as _____ during World War I.

7. The Navajo code was so effective, even _____ speakers of Navajo couldn't break it.

8. Their families at home put in a lot of _____ to support the men and women serving overseas.

9. The U.S. government used patriotic posters to _____ the men, women, and children on the home front to support the war.

10. Everyone made great _____ to support their country and their freedom.

Write two new sentences. Use a word from the box in each sentence.

11. _____

_____

12. _____

_____

Write a Narrative Paragraph

A narrative paragraph gives the events or tells the story of something that happened. It can tell about what a person did or had to do in a situation.

A narrative paragraph about what a person did in a situation should include:

- ✔ An introduction to the person
- ✔ What that person did
- ✔ Reasons he or she made that decision
- ✔ A concluding sentence that wraps up your paragraph

Read the prompt.

In this lesson, you have read about millions of men, women, and children who made personal sacrifices for something they thought was more important than themselves. Now you will write a paragraph about a sacrifice you or someone you know of has made to make something else happen or change. Your paragraph should tell who the person was, what the person gave up, why they made the sacrifice, what the person did, and how things turned out.

Plan Your Writing

Use the graphic organizer to think about your topic and take notes about what you will write.

Who was the person?

What did the person give up?

Why did the person make the sacrifice?

What did the person do?

How does the person feel about what he or she did?

Write Your Paragraph

On the lines below or on a computer, write your narrative paragraph.

_____

_____

_____

_____

_____

_____

_____

_____

_____

_____

Review Your Writing

Use this list to check your writing.

- ☐ I told about a person who made a sacrifice.
- ☐ I described what the person did.
- ☐ I gave reasons for what the person did.
- ☐ I wrote a concluding sentence.
- ☐ I checked capitalization and spelling.

For practice with shifts in tense, complete the Language Skills Mini-Lesson on page 138.

After you check your work, make any corrections. Read your paragraph aloud to a partner. Listen to your partner's paragraph. Discuss what you want to know more about.

Think and Discuss

The United States Office of War Information created and printed over 200,000 poster designs during World War II. The posters that were made for the home front were to make Americans feel patriotic and to encourage them to become part of the war effort through rationing and saving.

Work in groups and talk about the effectiveness of the three World War II posters in this lesson. Talk about why you think each poster was created and if you think it did a good job. Why are posters like these sometimes called "weapons on the walls?"

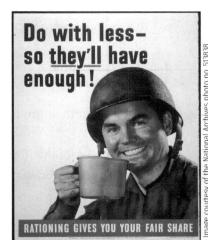

Image courtesy of the National Archives photo no. 513838

This poster was designed to support rationing at home.

Read the two selections. Circle the best answer to each question.

Text 1: An article about the Titanic

1   In April 1912, the Titanic set sail for New York. It was the ship's first trip across the Atlantic Ocean. It carried more than 2,200 people. Many famous and wealthy people were onboard. The ship had many comforts. It also had many safety features. Some people claimed the ship was unsinkable.

2   Just before midnight on April 14, the ship hit an iceberg. Water began to pour in. The crew loaded women and children into lifeboats. However, the lifeboats could hold only 1,200 people. Some were not full when they were put in the water. By 2 a.m., the ship had sunk. Hundreds of passengers and crew went with it. Those in lifeboats waited hours in the cold to be rescued. Only 705 people survived.

Text 2: Adapted from "When the Titanic Went Down," an account by passenger Elizabeth Shutes, 1913

1   Suddenly a strange quivering ran under the whole length of the ship. I sprang to the floor. With too perfect a trust in that mighty vessel I again lay down. Someone knocked at my door, and the voice of a friend said: "Come quickly to my cabin; an iceberg has just passed our window; I know we have just struck one." Why get dressed, as no one had given the slightest hint of any possible danger?

2   We left from the Sun Deck, 75 feet above the water. Two brave men saw us to the lifeboat, made no effort to save themselves. We were told to hunt under seats, anywhere, for a lantern, a light of any kind. Every place was empty. There was no water. Not a biscuit—nothing to keep us alive had we drifted long. Sitting by me in the lifeboat were a mother and daughter. The mother had left a husband on the Titanic, and the daughter a father and husband. These brave women never lost courage, forgot their own sorrow, telling me to sit close to them to keep warm. . . . The night was bitter cold, and it grew colder and colder. Just before dawn, the coldest, darkest hour of all, no help seemed possible.

1. What is the author's purpose in Text 1?
    a. to explain the safety features on the Titanic
    b. to tell what it felt like to be on a sinking ship
    c. to give information about what happened to the Titanic
    d. to describe what it was like to sail across the Atlantic in 1912

2. Why was Elizabeth Shute probably not worried at first?
    a. Her friend explained what had happened.
    b. The ship had survived hitting other icebergs.
    c. She was sleeping and didn't want to be bothered.
    d. She did not believe the ship could sink.

3. What does Elizabeth Shutes's account help you understand?
    a. the courage and strength of the survivors
    b. the unfairness that women and children were put on lifeboats first
    c. the reasons the Titanic sank
    d. the importance of having enough lifeboats

4. Which is the main idea of paragraph 2 in Text 1?
    a. The lifeboats on the ship could hold a total of 1,200 people.
    b. Only 705 people survived when the ship hit an iceberg and sank.
    c. The Titanic was supposed to be unsinkable, but it sank in a couple of hours.
    d. Women and children in lifeboats waited hours to be rescued.

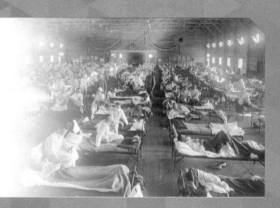

Disease Strikes the World

In this lesson, you will

READ

two passages about diseases in history:

- The Black Death
- The 1918 Flu Pandemic

USE THIS READING SKILL

Synthesize

USE THIS VOCABULARY SKILL

Understand words with the root *bio*

USE THIS WRITING SKILL

Write an explanatory text

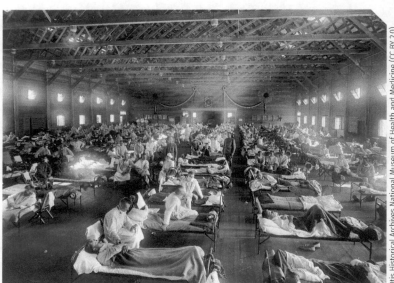

USE THESE KEY VOCABULARY WORDS

appear to begin to be seen

contagious having an illness that can be passed to someone else

origin the place where someone or something comes from

overwhelm to cause someone to have too many things to deal with

rapid happening quickly

realize to become aware of something

report to give information about something you have seen or done

resident a person who lives in a particular place

symptom a change in your body that shows you are sick

thrive to grow strong and healthy and succeed

UNDERSTAND THESE CONTENT VOCABULARY WORDS

antibiotics drugs that kill bacteria and stop infections

bacteria very small living things that often cause disease

censorship the act of examining and controlling content that is considered harmful to society

influenza (flu) an illness caused by a virus that can cause fever and pain

pandemic a time when a disease spreads quickly across a large area

plague a disease that kills many people

Use the Vocabulary

Answer these questions about the vocabulary words. Use the definitions on page 72 to help you.

1. What are some **symptoms** that would make you call a doctor?

   _____

2. What are some things that could make a student feel **overwhelmed**?

   _____

3. If you could be a **resident** of a different state or country, what place would you pick? Why?

   _____

4. If you had to **report** on what you have done during the past year, what would you **report**?

   _____

5. What does a plant need in order to **thrive**? What does a child need to **thrive**?

   _____

6. What would you do if smoke **appeared** in the hallway? Why?

   _____

7. What should someone do if they have a **contagious** disease?

   _____

8. What do you know about your family's **origin**?

   _____

9. What are some things that might give you a **rapid** heart rate?

   _____

10. When did you **realize** you wanted to go back to school?

    _____

VOCABULARY TIP

If you look a word up in the dictionary, it may have multiple meanings. Look at these definitions for the verb *appear*:

appear (verb)

   a. to seem   **b.** to begin to be seen   **c.** to show up   **d.** to be seen by the public

Write the letter of the definition that matches how *appear* is used in each sentence.

_____ **1.** Two cats appear at my door every morning looking for food.

_____ **2.** Some famous actors appear in that movie.

_____ **3.** It appears that he will win the election by only a few votes.

_____ **4.** As the sun came up, fog appeared on the mountain.

Preview

Preview the article to understand what you will learn. When you preview, read the title, first sentence, and headings. Look at any visuals, like maps or charts.

1. What is this article about? _____

2. What do the headings tell about? _____

3. What is the map about? _____

Take Notes

Taking notes about important ideas and information can help you understand and remember what you read.

Read the article. As you read, take notes about important ideas.

The Black Death

Underline the sentence that tells how many people died.

1 In the mid-1300s, a horrible disease spread through Europe. Sick people got egg-sized lumps under their arms. Then ugly black spots **appeared** on their skin. Other **symptoms**, such as fever, vomiting, and pain, followed. Most sick people died within a few days. Carts came through the streets to collect the dead. The disease was called the Black Death. It struck both rich and poor, big cities and small villages. In just a few years, around 25 million people in Europe died, about one-third of its population.

The Disease Arrives in Europe

Write a note about how and where plague arrived in Europe.

2 Many scientists today think the Black Death was bubonic plague, which is caused by a kind of bacteria. Around 1330, bubonic plague spread along trade routes from China. It killed millions. In 1347, ships carrying goods from Asia arrived at Messina on the island of Sicily. Many of the sailors were dead. Others were sick and covered in black sores. When citizens **realized** the ships carried disease, they ordered them away. But it was too late. The Black Death had arrived in Europe.

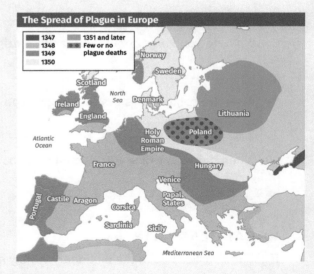

The Spread of Plague in Europe

3 Fearing the disease, some **residents** of Messina fled to other towns, carrying the plague with them. The ships that had been turned away landed at other ports, spreading the disease along trade routes. Other ships contributed to the **rapid** spread of plague throughout Europe.

How It Spread

Write a note about how plague spread.

4 Scientists think rats were the main way the plague spread. Rats and fleas were common in the 1300s. Rats **thrived** on ships and in filthy, crowded towns. When fleas bit an infected rat, they spread the bacteria to the next rat they bit. When the rats died, the fleas found human hosts. A single flea bite could infect a human.

5 People did not understand the disease. Some thought it was caused by bad air or the movement of the planets. Others thought it was punishment from God. There were no cures.

Write a note about what people thought caused plague.

More Outbreaks

6 Outbreaks of bubonic plague continued from the 1300s to the 1600s, but none were as severe as the Black Death. Plague still occurs today. Today, however, doctors can treat it quickly with antibiotics.

Check Your Comprehension

Answer these questions about the article.

1. What was the Black Death? _____

2. How did the Black Death come to Europe? _____

3. Look at the map. What can you tell about how bubonic plague spread in Europe? _____

_____

Synthesize

When you synthesize, you put the most important pieces of information from a text together to form a new understanding based on the information.

Use paragraph 1 to answer these questions. Use the information to draw conclusions and form a new understanding.

1. According to paragraph 1, what happened to someone who got the disease? _____

_____

2. How quickly did people die? _____

3. Carts collected the dead bodies. What does this help you understand?

_____

4. What conclusion can you draw based on the information in paragraph 1?

_____

> **TIP**
> When you draw a conclusion, you use information in the text and make a judgment about its meaning.

Use paragraphs 2 and 3 to answer these questions.

5. How did bubonic plague spread from China? _____

6. Why did the plague outbreak in Europe start on the island of Sicily? _____

_____

7. What can you conclude about how the plague spread? _____

_____

Use paragraph 4 to answer these questions.

8. What helped spread plague? _____

9. What conditions did rats like to live in? _____

10. How did conditions make it easier for the Black Death to spread? _____

IMPROVE YOUR READING

Read paragraph 1 silently. Pay attention to words you do not know. Break these words into parts and sound them out. Say hard words several times. Take turns with a partner reading the paragraph aloud.

Practice the Skills

Preview the article. Answer the questions.

1. Read the title. What will this article be about? _____

2. Look at the headings. What will the parts of this article be about?

   _____

3. Look at the advertisement and read the caption. What does the photo show?

   _____

Read the article. Use the prompts in the margin to take notes as you read.

The 1918 Flu Pandemic

INFLUENZA
Spread by Droplets sprayed from Nose and Throat

During the flu outbreak, some towns required people to wear masks in public to try to stop the spread of flu.

Image courtesy of the Library of Congress Prints and Photographs Division.

Make a note about how many people died.

1   In 1918, a highly **contagious** illness broke out. It was a severe and deadly type of flu. It struck quickly. In some cases, people died within hours of the first symptoms showing up. Hospitals were **overwhelmed** by the sick. Towns ran out of coffins. Bodies had to be buried in mass graves. In just 15 months, the flu killed between 50 million and 100 million people. It was the deadliest outbreak of disease in history.

The First Wave

Make a note about what happened in March 1918.

2   The **origin** of the 1918 flu may have been the United States. In March 1918, the country was fighting in World War I. At Camp Funston in Kansas, a military training camp, a soldier became ill. Within two days, 522 men **reported** illness. The first wave of the pandemic had begun.

3   Doctors were surprised. This new flu killed mostly young adults aged 20 to 40. Other flus killed mainly the very young, old, or sick.

How It Spread

Underline the sentence that tells how flu spreads.

4   Flu virus spreads in droplets when a sick person coughs, sneezes, or talks. The droplets can travel six feet away. People can also get sick by touching their face after handling something with the virus on it.

5   In April 1918, 118,000 American soldiers were sent to Europe. Some carried the flu virus with them. Soldiers were weakened by the stress of war, and they fought close together in dirty trenches. This caused the flu to spread rapidly among troops of all nations.

6   By summer, the flu had moved beyond the U.S. and Europe. New cases were reported in North Africa, India, and parts of Asia. Even so, officials thought the worst was over.

The Second Wave

Make a note about what happened in August 1918.

7   In late August 1918, a second, deadlier wave of the flu hit. At an army training base near Boston, 1,500 soldiers became ill in a single day. Doctors, nurses, and other workers were also sick. Without enough staff, the hospital stopped accepting patients. Thousands of other soldiers were sick and dying. Similar outbreaks happened in other cities.

Make a note about what helped flu spread

8   The country being at war made the problem worse. The military took many doctors and other medical workers. This left fewer staff to treat the public. Governments tried to hide the truth. Wartime censorship meant that outbreaks were not reported. To prevent panic, some health officials claimed the disease was under control.

9   During the worst part of the pandemic, schools and businesses closed. People stayed home. But by early 1919, the pandemic was ending. The war was over, and life returned to normal.

Check Your Comprehension

Answer these questions about the article.

1. What kind of illness is this article about? _____

2. How did the flu move from the United States to Europe? _____

3. What does the advertisement suggest? _____

Practice Synthesizing

When you synthesize, you combine facts and details from a text and put the information together to form a new understanding of an event. A graphic organizer can help summarize the most important information in a text and think about its significance.

HINT
Identify the main idea and the most important details in each section of text.

Complete the graphic organizer with important facts from the article. Use the information to draw conclusions about the flu pandemic. The first part has been done for you.

PARAGRAPHS	IMPORTANT INFORMATION	CONCLUSION BASED ON THE INFORMATION
1	50 million – 100 million people were killed in just over 15 months; the flu struck quickly	The amount of death must have been shocking and caused a lot of fear.
2–3	1.	2.
4–6	3.	4.
7–9	5.	6.
SYNTHESIS / OVERALL CONCLUSION		
7.		

IMPROVE YOUR READING

Read paragraphs 2 and 3 silently. Pay attention to the dates and numbers. Practice saying them. Then take turns reading the paragraphs aloud to a partner.

Respond to the Readings

Answer these questions about the articles.

1. What is the main idea of the article "The Black Death"?
   a. In the 1300s, people lived in filthy conditions, and rats were a common sight.
   b. People with bubonic plague could get lumps under their arms, black spots on their skin, fevers, and pain.
   c. The plague spread to Europe along trade routes and was carried by rats that thrived on ships and in dirty cities.

2. Why were people probably fearful of the Black Death? _____

   _____

3. Why did the 1918 flu pandemic have such a big impact? _____

   _____

4. Why might outbreaks of the flu have been connected to the military? Use what you learned about how flu spreads.

   _____

5. In what ways were the Black Death and the 1918 flu pandemic similar? _____

   _____

Use Word Parts: Root *bio*

Knowing the meaning of roots, prefixes, and suffixes can help you figure out the meaning of words. The root *bio* means "life." The word *antibiotics* has this root and means "a drug used to kill live bacteria."

Match the words from the box with their definitions below. Use a dictionary if you don't know the meaning of a word.

autobiography	biodiversity	biographer	biohazard	biology	biosphere

1. _____ the part of Earth that supports life

2. _____ a living thing that is dangerous to humans or the environment

3. _____ a person who writes the story of someone's life

4. _____ the science that studies life

5. _____ the written story of a person's own life

6. _____ many different kinds of living things in an environment

HINT
Look for word parts you know. The suffix *-er* means "a person who."

Review the Vocabulary

Read each group of words. Write the vocabulary word from the box that best goes with each group of words.

appear	contagious	origin	overwhelmed	rapid
realize	report	residents	symptom	thrive

1. to grow, to succeed, to prosper _____

2. to inform, to describe, to tell _____

3. beginning, start, source _____

4. quick, fast, speedy _____

5. a fever, a soar throat, a runny nose _____

Complete each sentence with a word from the box.

6. If you touch a poison ivy plant, a rash will _____ on your skin in 24 to 72 hours.

7. I picked up someone else's umbrella, but I did not _____ my mistake until I got home.

8. After the fire, the _____ of the apartment building had to find other places to live.

9. Troy felt _____ when he saw how much work had to be done in a very short time.

10. It's easy for young children at a day care to spread _____ diseases because they touch the same toys.

Write two new sentences. Use a word from the box in each sentence.

11. _____

_____

12. _____

_____

Write an Explanatory Text

The purpose of an explanatory text is to increase a reader's knowledge, to explain how something works, or to increase the reader's understanding of a concept. An explanatory text may give facts, details, and examples. Explanatory writing does not try to persuade or change a reader's thinking.

An explanatory text should include:

- ✓ A sentence that tells your main idea
- ✓ Specific details about the topic, such as facts, definitions, and examples
- ✓ Words and phrases that link information and ideas, such as *for example*, *also*, *because*, and *another reason*
- ✓ A concluding statement that summarizes the main points

Read the prompt.

> You have read two articles about major diseases in history. Which disease do you think was worse? Choose either the bubonic plaque or the 1918 flu and explain why it was a terrible disease. Use specific details and evidence from the article to develop your topic.

Plan Your Writing

Before you begin writing, review each article. Collect information about each disease and write it in the graphic organizer. Choose the disease you would like to write about. Use the notes in the graphic organizer to develop your ideas.

	BUBONIC PLAGUE	INFLUENZA
How many people were killed by the disease?		
How long did the outbreak of disease last?		
How did the disease get from one place to another?		
How was the disease transmitted?		
How was the disease able to spread so easily?		
Why was it hard for people to deal with the disease?		
What did people know about the disease / How did they try to stop it?		

Write Your Explanatory Text

On the lines below or on a computer, write your explanatory text.

TIP
Your first sentence should capture the reader's attention.

_____

_____

_____

_____

_____

_____

_____

Review Your Writing

Use this list to check your writing.

- ☐ I clearly state the topic I am writing about.
- ☐ I develop my topic with specific details and information.
- ☐ I organized my writing into paragraphs.
- ☐ I used words that link information.
- ☐ I wrote a conclusion.
- ☐ I checked the spelling and punctuation.

For practice with commas, complete the Language Skills Mini-Lesson on page 139.

After you check your work, make any corrections. Read your text aloud to a partner. Listen to your partner's text and ask you partner any questions you have.

Think and Discuss

During the flu pandemic, officials closed places like schools, theaters, and churches to try to stop the spread of the disease. Read the quote and look at the picture.

"It kept people apart. . . . You had no school life, you had no church life, you had nothing. . . . It completely destroyed all family and community life. . . . The terrifying aspect was when each day dawned you didn't know whether you would be there when the sun set that day."

— William Sardo, Washington, D.C.

How do you think the 1918 flu pandemic affected people's lives? How might people have felt when being around others in public? Talk about these questions in small groups.

Front page, The Seattle Times, October 5, 1918 (PD-US)

Invasive Species

In this lesson, you will

READ
two passages about invasive species:
- Animal Invaders
- Insect Invaders

USE THIS READING SKILL
Compare and contrast

USE THIS VOCABULARY SKILL
Understand words with the root *rupt*

USE THIS WRITING SKILL
Write a report

The kudzu vine spreads easily.

USE THESE KEY VOCABULARY WORDS

aggressive angry; ready to attack

decline to become worse in quality or fewer in number

disrupt to make it difficult for something to continue; to stop progress

disturb to bother; to change the position of something

impact influence or effect

import to bring something from one country to another

intentional done in a way that is planned; on purpose

invasive tending to spread easily

potential a chance that something will happen in the future

undetected not noticed or seen

UNDERSTAND THESE CONTENT VOCABULARY WORDS

cargo goods carried in a ship

ecosystem all the plants and living things in an environment

infected sick with something that causes disease

native existing naturally in a place

species a group of animals or plants that are related

Use the Vocabulary

Answer these questions about the vocabulary words. Use the definitions on page 82 to help you.

1. What are some things that could **disrupt** your sleep?

    _____

2. What kinds of products do you buy that are **imported** from another country?

    _____

3. What might cause a student's grades to **decline**?

    _____

4. What do you do when someone is driving **aggressively**? Why?

    _____

5. What people have had the biggest **impact** in your life?

    _____

6. What will probably happen if you **disturb** a beehive?

    _____

7. What would you do if **invasive** bugs came into the classroom?

    _____

8. How would you enter a room if you wanted to be **undetected**?

    _____

9. What do you think it means when someone **intentionally** slams a door?

    _____

10. What can you do to increase your **potential** to do well in a class?

    _____

VOCABULARY TIP

If you read a word you don't know, look for clues in nearby sentences. Sometimes authors will use an antonym, or a word that means the opposite, of an unknown word.

Read these sentences. Look for a word that means the opposite of declined.

*The amount in Barb's savings account **declined** last year. To fix the problem, she plans to look for a new job and reduce her spending. She hopes these changes will increase her savings.*

Which word means about the opposite of *declined*?

a. fix

b. plans

c. reduce

d. increase

Set a Purpose for Reading

Before you read the article, think about what you want to learn. Start by looking at the title, headings, and photos. Skim the article. Then look at the questions on page 85.

1. What are you going to be reading about? _____

2. What do the photos and captions help you understand? _____

3. Based on the questions on page 85, what should you look for as you read? _____

Make Connections

As you read, make connections to information in the text. You can make connections between ideas in the text and between things you have seen or read about.

Read the article. As you read, make connections to the ideas in the text. Answer the questions in the margin.

Animal Invaders

> What connection can you make to these plants and animals?

1   Americans benefit from many plants and animals that are not from here. For example, wheat, apples, cattle, and honeybees are not native to North America, but they are all valuable. Other kinds of plants and animals are not so welcome. Some species are **invasive**. This means they adapt to their new home, spread easily, and cause harm. Invasive species can hurt both the environment and the economy.

How Did They Get Here?

> Why might a pet owner release an animal into the wild?

2   Invasive species arrive in different ways. Some were brought on purpose. Animals like the red lionfish were brought as pets. Owners released them into the wild. The kudzu vine was **imported** and planted to give shade. Now these vines grow wild in the south. Similarly, fish like grass carp were brought for a reason. Fish farms brought them to control weeds. Now they have taken over entire rivers.

3   Other species came by accident. Zebra mussels arrived in seawater on cargo ships from overseas. Once in the U.S., they spread rapidly. Insect pests also got a ride on ships.

Burmese Pythons

> How does this snake compare to other snakes you have seen?

4   One of the most well-known invasive species is a reptile: the Burmese python. These large snakes from Asia can grow to be 20 feet long. These snakes were kept as pets and were released, either accidentally or on purpose, into the wild in Florida. Now 30,000 to 80,000 may live in the wild.

Burmese python

5   Pythons have had a big **impact** on the Florida Everglades ecosystem. They thrive in these warm swamplands and have few predators. They hunt all kinds of native wildlife, including deer, birds, rabbits, bobcats, and even alligators. Populations of some of these animals have **declined** up to 99 percent.

Wild Hogs

> **TIP**
> Wild hogs are also called wild boars and feral pigs.

6   Like pythons, hogs were brought to the U.S. **intentionally**. Early European settlers brought pigs with them. Some let their pigs roam freely until they wanted to eat them. But some pigs became wild. As many as 2 million to 6 million wild hogs now live in 39 U.S. states.

> How are wild hogs different from other pigs you have seen or know about?

7   Today, wild hogs are a huge problem. Like pythons, they lack natural predators. They can adapt easily. They eat almost anything, often destroying crops. They can also **disrupt** ecosystems. They eat nuts and seeds that other animals depend on. Their digging can cause soil erosion and make streams muddy.

Wild hogs

Check Your Comprehension

Answer these questions about the article.

1. What is an invasive species? _____

2. How do invasive species get here? _____

3. How did pythons and wild hogs get here? _____

Compare and Contrast

A writer may compare and contrast two people, events, things, or ideas. When you compare, you show how things are alike. When you contrast, you show how things are different.

Sometimes an author will directly state how things are alike or different. They may use words and phrase like these:

> **Words That Compare:** *like, alike, similar, both, also, similarly, same, just as, compared to*
> **Words That Contrast:** *differ, different, unlike, but, on the other hand, instead, in contrast*

Authors don't always state all the ways things are alike or different. Sometimes you will need to infer ways that two topics are alike and different.

Reread paragraph 1. Then answer the questions.

1. What are the examples of valuable plants and animals? _____

2. What are the valuable plants and animals contrasted with? _____

3. What are the two main things that invasive species hurt? _____

Answer these questions using paragraphs 2 and 3.

4. Underline words that compare or contrast. What words did you underline? _____

5. In what way are red lionfish, the kudzu vine, and grass carp alike? _____

6. How are zebra mussels and insect pests alike? _____

Answer these questions using paragraphs 4–7.

7. What are two ways Burmese pythons and wild hogs are alike? _____

    _____

8. What are two ways Burmese pythons and wild hogs are different? _____

    _____

9. Compare how many Burmese pythons and wild hogs are in the United States. _____

10. Which animal lives in more parts of the United States? How do you know? _____

HINT
You may have to infer information. For example, the article says pythons are reptiles. What kind of animal are pigs?

 Fluency **IMPROVE YOUR READING**

Practice reading paragraph 4 of "Animal Invaders" silently. As you read, pay attention to punctuation marks. Pause at the colon and commas. Take turns with a partner reading the paragraph aloud.

Practice the Skills

Set a purpose before you begin reading. Answer the questions.

1. What is this article going to be about? _____

2. Look at the maps. What do they show? _____

3. Read the questions on page 87. What should you look for as you read? _____

Read the article. As you read, make connections to what you know, what you've read, and what you've seen.

What connection can you make to insects you have seen?

How do mosquitoes spread disease?

What are the ants you have seen like? How do these ants compare?

TIP
25 mm = about 1 inch

What do you know about trees? Why would tunnels in the wood be harmful?

Insect Invaders

1 Insects are some of the worst invasive species in the U.S. Most are transported by accident. Their small size makes it easy for them to hide **undetected** inside wood, food, soil, and water. A few invasive insects, like gypsy moths, were brought on purpose.

2 Regardless of how they arrive, invasive insect species can be a big problem. They can cause economic harm. Insect pests can cause $13 billion in lost crops and $2 billion in forest damage per year. Insect pests can also cause health problems. For example, the Asian tiger mosquito can spread disease. Invasive insects can also hurt ecosystems. They might kill plants that other animals need for food or habitat.

Red Imported Fire Ants

3 Red imported fire ants first came to the U.S. in the 1930s by accident. The ants are native to South America. They arrived by ship in Mobile, Alabama. Since then, these pests have spread through nine southeastern states. Scientists believe they have the **potential** to spread even farther.

4 Fire ants are only 2 to 6 mm long, but they are **aggressive** and have painful stings. They attack anything that **disturbs** or comes near their nest. The ants lock on with strong jaws and sting repeatedly, causing blisters. The ants attack people. They can sting and even kill farm animals, pets, and wildlife. They can also damage crops and trees. Unfortunately, fire ants are hard to get rid of. They spread easily, moving in soil and on plants and even floating on flood waters.

Asian Long-Horned Beetles

5 Like fire ants, Asian long-horned beetles came to the U.S. by accident. However, these insects are large, 20 to 35 mm long, and are native to Asia. Scientists believe the insects arrived in 1996. They are believed to have come to New York inside the wood of packing crates.

6 Unlike fire ants, Asian long-horned beetles don't attack people or animals. Instead, they harm hardwood trees like maples. The beetle's larvae dig into the middle of the tree. This leaves big tunnels that weaken the tree. Adult beetles come out, leaving big holes in the bark. The trees are destroyed. The beetles slowly spread to nearby trees, so infected trees must be removed.

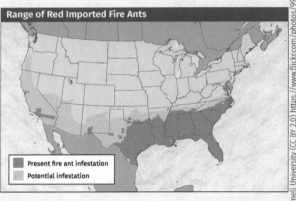

Range of Red Imported Fire Ants

- Present fire ant infestation
- Potential infestation

Asian Long-Horned Beetle Range

- Pest currently detected in this state
- At risk state

Check Your Comprehension

Answer these questions about the article.

1. Why are invasive insects a problem? _____

HINT
Reread paragraph 2.

2. What kind of harm do fire ants and Asian long-horned beetles cause? _____

3. What do the maps help you understand? _____

Practice Comparing and Contrasting

When you compare and contrast, you think about how things are alike and different. Sometimes an author will tell you ways that two things are alike and different. But other times, you need think about the information presented and find similarities and differences on your own.

A Venn diagram can help you compare and contrast two topics. A Venn diagram has two overlapping circles. In the left section below, you can write details about red imported fire ants. In the right section, you can write details about Asian long-horned beetles. In the middle section, where the circles overlap, you can write details that tell about both insects.

Fill in the missing information about the insects in the Venn diagram below. Then answer the question.

Red Imported Fire Ants

tiny size, 2–6 mm

1. _____

2. _____

came years ago, 1930s

affect mainly southern states

Both

insects

3. _____

4. _____

5. _____

Asian Long-Horned Beetles

6. _____

hurt trees

from Asia

7. _____

8. _____

9. Is this article more about comparing or contrasting the two insects? Explain your answer.

_____

_____

IMPROVE YOUR READING

Listen as your teacher reads paragraph 3 of "Insect Invaders" aloud. Pay attention to how your teacher groups words into phrases. Then read the paragraph out loud together as a class.

Respond to the Readings

Answer these questions about the articles.

1. Why is it a problem for Burmese pythons to live in the wild in Florida? _____

_____

2. There are from 2 million to 6 million wild hogs in the U.S. What does this help you understand about these animals?

_____

3. What is the main idea of "Insect Invaders"? _____

_____

4. What kinds of impacts might there be if Asian long-horned beetles spread?

_____

HINT
Of environmental, health, and economic impacts, which would the beetles most likely cause?

5. Which invasive species from the articles do you think is the most harmful? Why?

_____

TIP
The root *rupt* is always combined with other prefixes, suffixes, and roots to form words.

Use Word Parts: Root *rupt*

The word root *rupt* means "to break" or "to burst." The word *disrupt* has this root and can mean "to break apart."

Complete each sentence with a word from the box. Use a dictionary if you don't know the meaning of a word.

abrupt	bankrupt	corrupt	erupts	interruptions	rupture

1. When a volcano _____, it can send lava shooting into the air.

2. There were several _____ from the crowd during the president's speech.

3. I thought the movie had an _____ ending. It didn't resolve all the problems.

4. A company that loses all its money and can't pay what it owes is _____.

5. There was a _____ in the water pipeline, and water gushed down the street.

6. Kay lived in a country where a _____ leader stole money from the government.

Write your own sentences using these words. Use a dictionary if you need to.

7. disruption _____

8. corruption _____

Review the Vocabulary

Circle the letter of the answer that best completes each sentence.

1. _____ is something you would **import**.
   a. Your hair
   b. A friend
   c. A car

2. If a person has a health condition that is **undetected**, he _____.
   a. is very worried about it
   b. has had it for a long time
   c. doesn't know he has it

3. If a disease is **invasive**, it is _____.
   a. mild
   b. spreading
   c. easy to cure

4. An **aggressive** dog would probably _____.
   a. growl at you
   b. wag its tail
   c. lick your hand

Complete each sentence with a word from the box.

aggressive	decline	disrupt	disturb	impact
import	intentional	invasive	potential	undetected

5. Abby is just learning to play soccer, but she has the _____ to become a great player with practice and coaching.

6. When you plant a tree, you should be careful not to _____ the roots too much or you could damage them.

7. As people grow older, their eyesight can _____, so many older people don't like to drive at night.

8. I didn't invite Bret to the picnic, but it was not _____. I simply forgot to invite him.

9. The marathon course goes through downtown, and the race is going to _____ traffic all day.

10. When Diego lost his job, it had a big _____ on his family's budget.

Write two new sentences. Use a word from the box in each sentence.

11. _____

_____

12. _____

_____

Write a Report

A report is a kind of informational text. Its purpose is to increase a reader's knowledge about a topic. Reports are common in many aspects of life. For example, businesses might use reports to tell about a new product, a competitor, or a marketing plan. Governments issue reports on topics like housing, crime, and health. The content of reports can vary depending on their specific purpose and audience. They should include relevant facts and details.

A report should include:

- ✓ A clear statement of your topic
- ✓ Logical organization of your information, including sections and headings
- ✓ Specific information about your topic, including facts, details, and examples
- ✓ Precise language and vocabulary to inform about your topic

Read the prompt.

> Write a report about an invasive species. You may use one of the species in the readings or one of your choice. Use facts and information from the articles and from your own research.

Plan Your Writing

Before you begin writing, brainstorm ideas about an invasive species you will report on. Next, take notes from the article or from online sources to learn more about the species. Divide your notes into sections. Use the graphic organizer.

Invasive Species You Are Writing About
Physical Description of the Species
Impact of the Invasive Species
Origin and How It Came Here
Area Where It's Found
Information About How It Survives and What It Does

Write Your Report

On the lines below or on a computer, write your report.

TIP
Use headings to organize your details.

_____

_____

_____

_____

_____

_____

_____

_____

_____

Review Your Writing

Use this list to check your writing.

- ☐ I clearly stated my topic.
- ☐ I used headings to organize my information.
- ☐ I included facts, details, and examples.
- ☐ I used specific language.
- ☐ I checked the spelling and punctuation.
- ☐ I wrote complete sentences.

After you check your work, make any corrections. Read your report aloud to a partner. Listen to your partner's report and ask you partner any questions you have.

Think and Discuss

What factors do you think contribute to invasive species making it to the United States? What actions do you think governments and residents can take to reduce the impact they have?

Talk about these questions in small groups.

This sign warns boaters about zebra mussels.

Image courtesy of the Crow River Media

Too Little Rain, Too Much Rain

In this lesson, you will

READ

two passages about the weather:
- The Dust Bowl
- Mudslides

USE THIS READING SKILL

Identify sequence

USE THIS VOCABULARY SKILL

Understand words with the suffix *-en*

USE THIS WRITING SKILL

Write an informational text

USE THESE KEY VOCABULARY WORDS

abandon to leave and never return

absorb to take in liquid gradually and naturally

accumulate to gather or build up over time

collapse to fall down or inward

decade a period of 10 years

disaster a sudden event such as a flood or storm that causes harm or danger

drought a long period of dry weather when there is little or no rain

prone to likely to do something or suffer from something

region a fairly large area of a state, country, etc.

swirl to turn around and around

UNDERSTAND THESE CONTENT VOCABULARY WORDS

boulder a rock that is too large for a person to move

earthquake a sudden shaking of the earth's surface that often causes damage

erode to gradually wear away land due to wind or rain

flash flood a sudden local flood caused by heavy rain

logging the business of cutting down trees for wood, paper, etc.

plow to turn up the soil for planting

A farm is covered in dust during the Dust Bowl.

A building is pushed downhill in a mudslide.

Use the Vocabulary

Answer these questions about the vocabulary words. Use the definitions on page 92 to help you.

1. Would you adopt a dog that has been **abandoned**? Why or why not?

   _____

2. What **decade** were you born in?

   _____

3. What are two things in your home that **absorb** water well?

   _____

4. Name something your best friend is **prone to**.

   _____

5. What **region** of the country do you live in?

   _____

6. What things may **collapse** due to extreme weather?

   _____

7. What happens to trees and plants during a **drought**?

   _____

8. How do people change after they **accumulate** a lot of money?

   _____

9. Describe a **disaster** that you've experienced, read, or heard about.

   _____

10. What are three things that can **swirl** in the air?

   _____

VOCABULARY TIP

Some words have more than one meaning. To figure out the correct meaning of the word, look for clues in the text.

Read the sentences and look for clues about the meaning of *collapse*. Circle the correct definition.

*The large mudslides caused the **collapse** of over 100 homes. Rescuers had to dig through the damage to find people.*

   a. *(verb)* to break apart and fall down suddenly
   b. *(verb)* to fall down or become unconscious because you are ill or exhausted
   c. *(noun)* a complete failure or breakdown
   d. *(noun)* a situation in which something, suddenly breaks apart and falls down

Skim

Skimming is reading a text quickly to get a general idea of meaning. When you skim, read the title, the subheads, the charts or maps, and the sentences with bold words. Read the first paragraph and the last paragraph.

1. What is the title of the article? _____

2. What does the map show? _____

3. What is the article about? _____

Reread

Rereading can make you a better reader. It can help you better understand the article, understand new words, and find information you might have missed the first time. When you reread, go back far enough in the text to help you understand.

Read the article. If you get to a part that is difficult or contains important information, look back through the text and reread to gain understanding.

The Dust Bowl

1 In the 1930s, the United States experienced one of the worst environmental **disasters** in history. The Dust Bowl, also known as the Dirty '30s, was caused by ten years of **drought** conditions and poor land use. Tall prairie grass once covered the Great Plains. In the 1910s and 1920s, farmers plowed over more than five million acres of the native grass to grow wheat. Wheat was easy to grow and was needed around the world. When wheat prices fell in 1929 as a result of the Great Depression, many fields were **abandoned**.

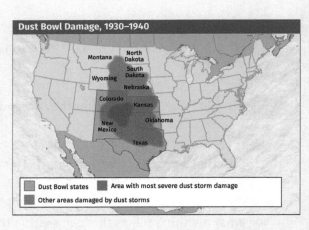

Dust Bowl Damage, 1930–1940

Montana, North Dakota, South Dakota, Wyoming, Nebraska, Colorado, Kansas, New Mexico, Oklahoma, Texas

- Dust Bowl states
- Area with most severe dust storm damage
- Other areas damaged by dust storms

2 Then, the Great Plains were hit by a number of severe droughts in the 1930s (1930–1931, 1934, 1936, and 1939–1940). The droughts killed off the remaining wheat. The empty fields had no grass to hold the dirt in place. High winds blew in and easily picked up the dirt and formed it into dust clouds. By 1935, approximately 260 million acres of land had lost or was about to lose all or most of its top layer of soil. Dust storms swept the Great Plains every year of that **decade**.

Why was the Dust Bowl also called the Dirty '30s? Reread the passage to help you with the answer.

3 The large dust storms, called "black blizzards," swept up millions of tons of dirt from the dry fields and **swirled** it up into the air. Clouds of dust were so big they could block out the sun, sometimes for days. Total blackouts lasted as long as 11 hours. Sometimes there was thunder and lightning. Occasionally, the dust storms piled up enough dirt to cover houses, cars, and animals. April 14, 1935, known as "Black Sunday," was the worst black blizzard of the Dirty '30s. More than 300,000 tons of dust traveled across the country to the East Coast. The winds blew up to 100 miles an hour. The dust cloud was over 1,000 miles long.

4 The government started to take action. Farmers learned smarter ways to plant and grow their crops. They learned how to keep their soil in place and how to prevent damage to the land. Over 220 million trees were planted across the Great Plains as protection from the wind.

5 The Dust Bowl that had begun with the drought of 1930 lasted throughout the decade and ended with the last drought of 1940. Its long-term economic effect on the Great Plains lasted much longer.

Check Your Comprehension

Answer these questions about the article.

1. When did the droughts begin? _____

2. What was Black Sunday? _____

3. Look at the map Dust Bowl Damage, 1930–1940. What does it show you? _____

Identify Sequence

Sequencing is recognizing the order in which events occur. There is a beginning, a middle, and an end. You use sequencing to retell events or explain a process. Each event leads to the next.

1. Reread paragraph 1. Number the events in the order they happened.

_____ **a.** The price of wheat fell.

_____ **b.** Farmers grew wheat on the prairies.

_____ **c.** The prairies were covered with native grasses.

_____ **d.** The Great Depression started in 1929.

2. Reread paragraph 2. Write three events in the order they happened. Use your own words.

   a. _____

   b. _____

   c. _____

3. Reread paragraph 3. Find two events in sequence. Write them here.

   a. _____

   b. _____

 IMPROVE YOUR READING

Practice reading paragraph 4 of "The Dust Bowl" silently. Then read it again, paying attention to punctuation and to how you can group words together into phrases. Take turns with a partner reading the paragraph aloud.

Practice the Skills

Skim the article. Answer the questions.

1. Read the title. What will this article be about? _____

2. What are landslides? _____

3. What does the graphic illustrate? _____

Read the article. Reread any difficult parts to understand things you might have missed in your first reading.

Mudslides

1 Landslides are when boulders, earth, or other debris move downhill. Mudslides are fast-moving landslides made of mud and other earthy material. Mudslides usually occur in areas where there are no trees or plants to hold the soil in place or to catch rain as it falls. The water rapidly **accumulates** in the ground and results in a powerful flow of loosened rock, earth, and debris that is filled with water. A reporter writing about 2018 California mudslides wrote that it's the type of mud that "will suck the boots right off your feet."

2 Mudslides (also called "debris flows") generally travel at 10 miles per hour, but can reach speeds of 35 miles per hour. They increase in size and speed as they pick up loose topsoil and any other materials in their way. In 2014, a debris flow in Oso, Washington, covered a square mile in about 20 seconds.

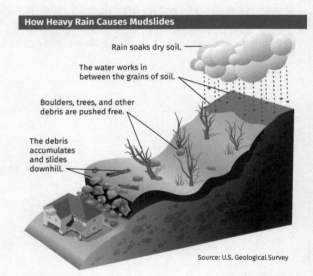

How Heavy Rain Causes Mudslides

Rain soaks dry soil.

The water works in between the grains of soil.

Boulders, trees, and other debris are pushed free.

The debris accumulates and slides downhill.

Source: U.S. Geological Survey

3 It's hard to predict when and where mudslides will happen. They can occur in every state at any time of the year, although they usually take place on the hillsides of the West Coast. The states of Washington, Oregon, California, Alaska, and Hawaii are **prone to** mudslides because of the earthquakes, rainfall, and wildfires that are common in the **region**.

Reread to determine why locations downhill and downstream from wildfires are prone to flash floods and mudslides.

4 Debris flows are most likely to happen in areas where people have built roads and buildings, where there has been logging, where landslides have occurred before, and where there have been recent wildfires. Mudslides usually follow other natural disasters, such as earthquakes and wildfires. Wildfires create "burn scars" where the ground is so burnt that the soil cannot **absorb** the rain. Locations downhill and downstream from a burn scar are open to flash flooding and mudslides.

5 In 2018, heavy rain created flash floods and debris flows in southern California. In 2017, the state had its worst wildfire season in history. The largest and final fire, called the Thomas fire, lasted for more than a month. It burned more than 280,000 acres. Just weeks after the Thomas fire ended, it rained. A half inch of rain fell in five minutes. This caused the land to **collapse** where there were no plants or trees to hold it in place. Mud, boulders, and tree branches moved downhill at speeds of up to 20 miles per hour.

Check Your Comprehension

Answer these questions about the article.

1. What is another name for a mudslide? _____

2. Where are mudslides most likely to occur in the United States? _____

3. What is a burn scar? _____

Practice Identifying Sequence

Sequence describes events in the order they happened, happen, or will happen. Sometimes the events are written in a text or in a chart. Sometimes they are illustrated.

1. Reread the illustration of how a heavy rain can cause a mudslide. Then put the events in the correct order.

_____ **a.** The debris accumulates and slides downhill

_____ **b.** Boulders, trees, and other debris are pushed free.

_____ **c.** Rain soaks the dry soil.

_____ **d.** The water works in between the grains of soil.

2. Reread paragraph 4. Complete the graphic organizer to show the sequence of events. You may not need to use all of the spaces. Sometimes events might not be written in the order they happen. Use clues in the text and what you know to infer the sequence of events.

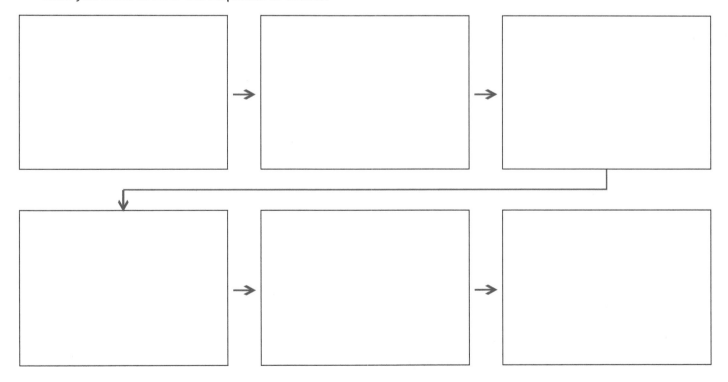

IMPROVE YOUR READING

Listen and read along silently as your teacher reads paragraph 1 of "Mudslides." Pay attention to your teacher's tone and expression. Then read the paragraph aloud with your teacher.

Respond to the Readings

Answer these questions about the articles.

TIP
Use the map on page 94 and the graphic on page 96 to help you answer the questions.

1. What were the geographic boundaries of the Dust Bowl? _____
_____

2. What caused the Dust Bowl? _____
_____

3. What is the difference between a landslide and a mudslide? _____
_____

4. What happens during a mudslide? _____
_____

5. What roles do people and nature have in causing the Dust Bowl and mudslides? _____
_____

Use Word Parts: Suffix -*en*

The suffix -*en* means "to make" or "to become." You can add -*en* to the end of some adjectives or nouns to make verbs. For example, when you add the suffix -*en* to the adjective *wide*, the new word is the verb *widen*. If the adjective or noun end in *e*, just add *n*.

Add the suffix -en to the adjectives or nouns in the first column. Use a dictionary to check your spelling.

TIP
The suffix -*en* can also be added to nouns to mean "made of" as in *golden* and *wooden*, but it is uncommon.

	+ -*en*			+ -*en*
1. bright			5. short	
2. dark			6. straight	
3. fright			7. sweet	
4. loose			8. worse	

Complete each sentence with a word from the boxes. Use each word only once. Use a dictionary if you don't know the meaning of a word.

9. After eating a big Thanksgiving dinner, many people have to _____ their belt.

10. Lynn's coffee was so bitter that she needed to _____ it with three spoonfuls of sugar.

11. You can _____ your day by being kind to someone else.

12. Spiders and snakes _____ Alan.

13. The clouds started to _____ as the storm moved closer.

14. Why don't you _____ the curtains so they don't touch the floor?

Review the Vocabulary

Read each group of words. Write the vocabulary word from the box that best goes with each group of words.

| abandon | absorb | accumulate | collapse | decade |
| disaster | drought | prone to | region | swirl |

1. take up, soak up, draw in _____

2. spiral, revolve, spin _____

3. break down, fall in, give way _____

4. failure, trouble, emergency _____

5. area, country, place _____

Complete each sentence with a word from the box.

6. The 1950s was the _____ of economic good times and rock and roll.

7. The 2008 _____ in Spain was so bad that the city of Barcelona bought water from France.

8. Many of the towns that people had to _____ in the 1930s are still empty ghost towns today.

9. Large piles of dust and sand would _____ around buildings, trucks, and cars, sometimes covering them completely.

10. Los Angeles, California, tops the list of U.S. cities most _____ drought.

Write two new sentences. Use a word from the box in each sentence.

11. _____

_____

12. _____

_____

Write an Informational Text

Informational texts share information about a topic. They contain facts, not opinions. You've seen examples of informational text when you read directions or an article in this book.

An informational text should include:

- ✓ A sentence that introduces your topic
- ✓ Information, facts, and details that relate to the topic
- ✓ Vocabulary and phrases that relate to the topic
- ✓ A concluding sentence that relates to your ideas

Read the prompt.

> Write an informational text explaining why droughts and mudslides are dangerous. Use information from your own experiences, from the articles in this lesson, and from additional internet research to support your ideas.

Plan Your Writing

Before you begin writing, think about what information you want to give your reader. Think about what a reader needs to know in order to understand the dangers of droughts and mudslides.

Use the graphic organizer below to organize your ideas. Put your ideas in the correct order.

Sentence that introduces your topic	
Idea 1	**Facts and details**
Idea 2	**Facts and details**
Idea 3	**Facts and details**
Concluding sentence	

Write an Informational Text

On the lines below or on a computer, write your informational text.

_____

_____

_____

_____

_____

_____

_____

_____

Review Your Writing

Use this list to check your writing.

- ☐ My first sentence tells the topic I am writing about.
- ☐ I presented information clearly.
- ☐ I included specific details, facts, and examples.
- ☐ I used vocabulary and phrases that relate to the topic.
- ☐ I checked the spelling and punctuation.

For practice with conditional sentences, complete the Language Skills Mini-Lesson on page 140.

After you check your work, make any corrections. Read your text aloud to a partner. Then discuss how your texts were similar and different.

Think and Discuss

The song "So Long, It's Been Good to Know Yuh!" was written by Woody Guthrie in 1935. Guthrie was living in the town of Pampa, in Gray County, Texas, during the Black Sunday dust storm. Here is the chorus and a verse from the song.

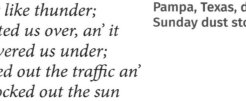

Pampa, Texas, during the Black Sunday dust storm

(Chorus)
So long, it's been good to know yuh;
So long, it's been good to know yuh;
So long, it's been good to know yuh
This dusty old dust is a-gettin' my home
And I got to be driftin' along.

A dust storm hit, an' it hit like thunder;
It dusted us over, an' it covered us under;
Blocked out the traffic an' blocked out the sun
Straight for home all the people did run.

What do these lyrics help you understand about Black Sunday?

Read the article. Circle the best answer to each question.

Physical Weathering

Weathering

1 Weathering breaks rocks down into smaller pieces such as pebbles, sand, and soil. When the smaller pieces are loosened and move, it is called erosion. There are three types of weathering: physical, chemical, and biological. Physical weathering is caused by changes in temperature, freezing and thawing, and the effects of wind, rain, and waves.

Temperature Changes

2 The sun can heat rocks to very high temperatures. When the rocks are hot, they expand. When the temperature drops, the rocks cool down and contract. If a rock is heated and cooled many times, cracks form, and pieces of rock wear off. This type of physical weathering happens a lot in deserts because the days are very hot and the nights get very cold.

Water collects in the crack of a rock.

Water freezes and expands. The crack widens.

The ice thaws and contracts. The water moves deeper into the crack.

Over time, the rock splits.

TIP
The word *thaws* means melts.

Freeze-Thaw

3 When water freezes, it expands. When water collects in the cracks of a rock and freezes, the cracks get bigger when the water expands. This can also cause new cracks to form. The water moves deeper into the cracks when the ice thaws. When the rock freezes again, that water expands and makes the cracks even bigger. The ice slowly widens the cracks and splits the rock. As this happens over and over, the rocks weaken and split and smaller pieces wear away. This type of physical weathering happens in cold climates.

The Wind and Moving Water

4 The power of the wind and moving water also cause physical weathering. They hit the rock over and over, causing it to break down into smaller pieces that get carried away by the wind or water. For example, when water in a river or stream moves quickly, it can lift up rocks from the bottom. When the rocks drop back down they bump into other rocks, and small pieces of the rocks can break apart.

1. Which sentence is a sequence?
   a. When the smaller pieces are loosened and move, it is called erosion.
   b. When the rock freezes again, that water expands and makes the cracks even bigger.
   c. This type of physical weathering happens in cold climates.
   d. The power of wind, waves, and rain also cause weathering.

2. According to the article, how is weathering caused by temperature changes and weathering caused by freeze-thaws alike?
   a. The sun heats rocks to very high temperatures.
   b. The water freezes and expands.
   c. They both happen in deserts.
   d. The weather gets cold.

3. The acid in rainwater can react with some rocks to cause weathering. What does this new information add to your understanding of weathering?
   a. Rainwater can cause weathering in several ways.
   b. The acid in rainwater is what makes ice thaw.
   c. Weathering requires water.
   d. Some types of rocks weather easily.

4. Which paragraph helps explain the Dust Bowl?
   a. paragraph 1
   b. paragraph 2
   c. paragraph 3
   d. paragraph 4

UNIT 4

Literature

The Open Boat

In this lesson, you will

READ

selections from the short story
- "The Open Boat," by Stephen Crane

USE THIS READING SKILL

Understand figurative language and imagery

USE THIS VOCABULARY SKILL

Understand words with the prefixes *super-* and *sur-*

USE THIS WRITING SKILL

Write a description

The SS Commodore

USE THESE KEY VOCABULARY WORDS

abrupt sudden and unexpected

comfortably easily; in a way that causes no unpleasant feelings

grace a way of moving that is smooth and elegant

grim looking serious; depressing

menace a threat; something that causes harm or danger

navigation the process of planning your route or steering a vehicle

outburst a sudden show of strong feeling

stationary still; not moving

survey to look carefully at and examine an area

temporarily in a way that lasts only a short time and is not permanent

UNDERSTAND THESE CONTENT VOCABULARY WORDS

figurative language words that have a meaning beyond their literal or ordinary meaning and that paint a picture for the reader

imagery the pictures that an author's words help paint in the reader's mind

metaphor a comparison between two unlike things that doesn't use the words *like* or *as*

personification giving human qualities to a nonhuman or nonliving thing

simile a comparison between two unlike things using the words *like* or *as*

Use the Vocabulary

Answer these questions about the vocabulary words. Use the definitions on page 104 to help you.

1. If you **surveyed** your classroom or your surroundings right now, what would you see?

   _____

2. If you had to **temporarily** give up something like a cellphone, car, or favorite food, which would be most difficult?

   _____

3. Do you think **navigation** of a car cross-country is easier or harder today than 100 years ago? Why?

   _____

4. What are some things that are a **menace** to your community? Explain.

   _____

5. Where is a place that you can read or study **comfortably**? What makes that a **comfortable** place?

   _____

6. Why might someone make an **abrupt** exit from a movie theater? Why might someone **abruptly** leave class?

   _____

7. Describe someone who moves with **grace**. What makes that person **graceful**?

   _____

8. Should professional athletes be fined when they have **outbursts** during games or matches? Explain.

   _____

9. Would you rather ride a **stationary** bike or a regular bike? Explain.

   _____

10. What might cause someone to have a **grim** look on their face?

   _____

VOCABULARY TIP

Some words have more than one meaning. To figure out the correct meaning, think about the context, or how the word is used in a sentence. Here are three definitions of *grace*.

a. smooth and pleasing movement

b. a prayer said before a meal

c. good manners and polite behavior

Read the sentences. Write the letter of the definition that matches how *grace* is used.

_____ **1.** Don showed grace and patience when dealing with the angry customer.

_____ **2.** We were amazed by the grace of the dancer's movements.

_____ **3.** The Smiths asked Tony to say grace before dinner.

Use Prior Knowledge

Thinking about your own knowledge and experiences can help you make sense of what you read. Start by reading the title of the selection. Think about what you know.

1. What is this story going to be about? _____

2. What do you already know about being on a small boat on the ocean from movies, TV shows, or your own

   experiences? _____

3. Based on what you know, what will the story probably describe? _____

Visualize

As you read, pay attention to the details in the selection. Think about why they are important. Use the details to create a picture in your mind.

As you read, visualize what the author describes. Answer the questions in the margin.

Adapted from "The Open Boat"
by Stephen Crane

> How do you picture the ocean in paragraph 1?

1 None of them knew the color of the sky. Their eyes were locked on the waves that swept toward them. These waves were the color of slate, except for the tops, which were foaming white. The horizon narrowed and widened, and dipped and rose. At all times its edge was jagged with waves that seemed thrust up in points like rocks.

2 A man ought to have a bathtub larger than the boat which here rode upon the sea. The waves were most **abrupt** and tall, and each froth-top was a problem in small boat **navigation**.

> **TIP**
> The *bow* is the front of a boat; the *stern* is the back. The pronoun *she* is sometimes used to refer to boats.

3 The cook crouched in the bottom and looked at the six inches of boat that separated him from the ocean. His sleeves were rolled over his fat forearms. The two flaps of his unbuttoned vest dangled as he bent to bail out the boat.

4 The oiler, steering with one of the two oars in the boat, sometimes raised himself suddenly to keep clear of water that swirled in over the stern.

5 The reporter, pulling at the other oar, watched the waves and wondered why he was there.

6 The injured captain, lying in the bow, was buried in the deep sadness that comes, **temporarily** at least, to even the bravest when the company fails, the army loses, or the ship goes down.

> What picture do you have in your mind about the boat and the men in it?

7 A seat in this boat was like a seat upon a bucking bronco, and a bronco is not much smaller. The boat pranced and reared and plunged like an animal. As each wave came, and the boat rose for it, the boat seemed like a horse leaping at a high fence. Her scramble over these walls of water is a mystic thing. The top of them required a new leap, and a leap from the air. Then, after bumping a crest, she would slide, and race, and splash down a long slope, and arrive bobbing in front of the next **menace**.

> Picture what is happening. What is the ocean like?

8 A problem with the sea is that after successfully overcoming one wave you discover that there is another behind it just as important and just as anxious to flood boats. As each slaty wall of water approached, it shut all else from the view of the men in the boat. It was easy to imagine that this particular wave was the final **outburst** of the ocean, the last effort of the **grim** water. There was a terrible **grace** in the movement of the waves. They came in silence, except for the snarling of the crests.

Check Your Comprehension

Answer these questions about the story.

1. Where does this part of the story take place? _____

2. Who are the characters in the story? _____

3. What does this part of the story describe? _____

Understand Figurative Language and Imagery

Authors use imagery and figurative language to paint a picture in a reader's mind. Imagery is the use of language and descriptions that appeal to our senses. Figurative language is the use of words outside of their literal, or ordinary, meaning. Similes, metaphors, and personification are examples of figurative language.

- A *simile* compares two unlike things using the words *like* or *as*: *His voice was like butter.*

- A *metaphor* compares two unlike things without using the words *like* or *as*: *The grass was a soft green carpet.*

- *Personification* gives human qualities to nonhuman things: *The sun peeked out from behind the clouds.*

Answer the questions about language and imagery in the story.

1. Reread the first sentence of the story. Why don't the men know the color of the sky?

   _____

   HINT
   Look at the next sentence. What does it mean when your eyes are "locked on" something?

2. In paragraph 1, what is happening with the men's view of the horizon?

   _____

3. What are the waves being compared to in the last sentence of paragraph 1? _____

4. Based on the details in paragraph 1, you can tell that the sea is
   a. calm
   b. loud
   c. rough

5. In paragraph 2, what does the author compare the size of the boat to? _____

6. What does this comparison in paragraph 2 help you understand about the boat? _____

7. What is the main simile in paragraph 7? _____

8. List four words from paragraph 7 that show how the boat is like a horse. _____

9. In paragraph 7, what does the author mean by the "next menace"? _____

   _____

10. In paragraph 8, what words show that the ocean is being personified, or given human qualities? Give three

    examples. _____

 IMPROVE YOUR READING

Work with a partner. Practice reading paragraph 7 silently. Pay attention to your speed and pacing. Then take turns reading the text aloud to your partner.

Practice the Skills

Think about what you already know before you begin reading. Answer the questions.

1. Based on the first excerpt, what is it like to be on the sea? _____

2. Look at the photograph of the lighthouse. What do you know about lighthouses? _____

3. Based on what you know and have read so far, what do you think will happen? _____

Read the selection. Visualize what is happening. Answer the questions in the margin.

Adapted from "The Open Boat"
by Stephen Crane

What do you picture in paragraph 1?

1 As the boat bounced from the top of each wave, the wind tore through the hair of the hatless men, and as the craft plopped her stern down again the spray slashed past them. The crest of each of these waves was a hill, from the top of which the men **surveyed**, for a moment, a wide area, shining and split by wind. It was probably splendid. It was probably glorious, this play of the free sea, wild with lights of emerald and white and amber.

Describe what you see in paragraph 2.

2 Gulls flew near and far. Sometimes they sat down on the sea, near patches of brown seaweed that rolled over the waves with a movement like carpets on a clothesline in a strong wind. The birds sat **comfortably** in groups. They were envied by some in the dinghy, for the anger of the sea was no more to them than it was to a bunch of chickens a thousand miles inland. Often they came very close and stared at the men with black bead-like eyes.

TIP
A *dinghy* is a small boat or lifeboat.

3 In the meantime the oiler and the reporter rowed. And also they rowed.

4 They sat together in the same seat, and each rowed an oar. Then the oiler took both oars; then the reporter took both oars; then the oiler; then the reporter. They rowed and they rowed.

5 The brown mats of seaweed that appeared from time to time were like islands, bits of earth. They were travelling, apparently, neither one way nor the other. They were, for all purposes, **stationary**. They let the men in the boat know that it was making progress slowly toward the land.

6 The captain, after the dinghy soared on a great wave, said that he had seen the lighthouse at Mosquito Inlet. Then the cook said that he had seen it. The reporter was at the oars then, and for some reason he too wished to look at the lighthouse. But his back was toward the far shore and the waves were important, and for some time he could not get a chance to turn his head.

What does the reporter see in paragraph 7?

7 But at last there came a wave more gentle than the others. His eyes chanced on a small still thing on the edge of the swaying horizon. It was exactly like the point of a pin. It took an eager eye to find a lighthouse so tiny.

8 "Think we'll make it, captain?"

9 "If this wind holds and the boat don't swamp, we can't do much else," said the captain.

Check Your Comprehension

Answer these questions about the story.

1. Besides the boat, what other things are floating on the ocean? _____

2. What are the men doing in this part of the story? _____

3. At the end of the excerpt, what do the men see? _____

Practice Understanding Figurative Language and Imagery

Figurative language and imagery help authors paint a picture in a reader's mind. The language can also help an author express a message in a story.

Answer the questions.

1. In the first sentence, what do the word choices *bounced*, *tore*, and *slashed* help you understand?

   _____

2. In paragraph 1, the author uses a metaphor to compare the top of the waves to

   a. spray   **b.** a hill   **c.** wind

3. In paragraphs 2 and 5, what two things does the author compare the seaweed to? _____

4. In paragraph 2, why might the men envy the gulls? _____

5. How is the experience of the men in the boat different from that of the gulls and the seaweed?

   _____

6. When the reporter does see the lighthouse, what does it look like? _____

7. What does this help you understand about the lighthouse? _____

Complete the graphic organizer with details from both excerpts describing the sea. Use the details to draw a conclusion about the author's message about nature.

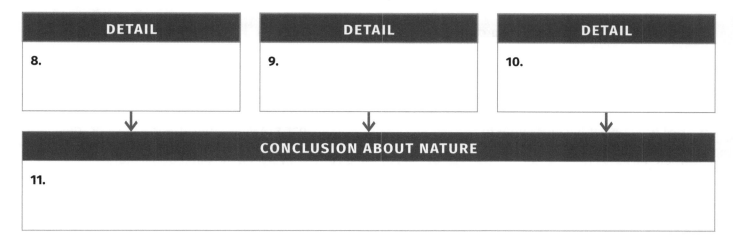

DETAIL	DETAIL	DETAIL
8.	9.	10.

CONCLUSION ABOUT NATURE
11.

 IMPROVE YOUR READING

Read paragraphs 3 and 4 silently. As you read, focus on punctuation and grouping words together in phrases. Work with a partner. Take turns reading the paragraphs aloud.

Respond to the Readings

Answer these questions about the story.

1. Which of these is the main conflict or problem in the story?

   a. man against himself

   b. man against man

   c. man against nature

2. In the second excerpt, the author writes that the view of the sea from the boat was "probably splendid" and "probably glorious." What do you think the author means by this?

   _____

3. Are the people and events in this story more realistic or more imaginary? Explain.

   _____

4. Do you think the reporter is excited or disappointed when he spots the lighthouse? Explain your answer.

   _____

5. At the end of the second excerpt, the captain says he thinks the boat will make it to the lighthouse if the wind keeps blowing and the boat doesn't swamp. Based on the how nature has been shown so far in the story, do you think they will make it? Explain your answer.

   _____

Use Word Parts: Prefixes *super-* and *sur-*

The prefixes *super-* and *sur-* can mean "on top of; over; above; beyond." For example, when you survey land, you look over it. A supermarket is above or beyond a regular market.

Complete each sentence with a word from the box. Use a dictionary if you don't know the meaning of a word.

supersize	supervises	surcharge	surface	surpassed	surplus

1. Last month, my cable bill had a $10 _____ for sports channels.

2. The _____ of the lake was as smooth as glass on the mild spring day.

3. Fast food restaurants may offer to _____ parts of your order, like the drink or fries.

4. There was a _____ of food at the picnic, so everyone took home some leftovers.

5. Maggie _____ three workers at the hotel.

6. This year's peach crop _____ last year's crop, which was damaged by storms.

Write your own sentences using these words. Use a dictionary if you need to.

7. superior _____

8. surround _____

Review the Vocabulary

Circle the letter of the answer that best completes the sentence.

1. If you see a bird outside and it is **stationary**, it is _____.
   a. still
   b. singing
   c. colorful

2. For help with **navigation**, you could use _____.
   a. water
   b. a map
   c. a ruler

3. _____ would be considered a **menace**.
   a. A difficult homework assignment
   b. A crawling baby
   c. A snarling wild animal

4. If you **survey** the contents of a refrigerator, you _____.
   a. observe what is there
   b. throw things away
   c. make yourself a snack

5. If you are working somewhere **temporarily**, you are _____.
   a. working a lot of hours
   b. earning a lot of money
   c. working for a short time

6. A person who moves with **grace** moves _____.
   a. sadly
   b. quickly
   c. smoothly

Complete each sentence with a word from the box.

abrupt	comfortably	grace	grim	menace
navigation	outburst	stationary	survey	temporarily

7. There was an _____ change in weather. The temperature dropped 30 degrees in an hour.

8. The judge warned people in the courtroom to be quiet, but there was an _____ when the verdict was read.

9. Tim is feeling better, and he is resting _____ at home after the accident.

10. Mr. Wilson had a _____ look on his face when he heard that his car had been stolen.

Write two new sentences. Use a word from the box in each sentence.

11. _____

_____

12. _____

_____

Write a Description

Descriptive writing uses sensory details. Good descriptions can help bring a writer's subject alive in the minds of readers. Strong descriptions can be found in fiction and literature, but it can also be an important part of informational text and persuasive writing. For example, an article about a sports event might include strong descriptions and sensory details. Persuasive writing forms, such as advertisements, also rely on strong descriptions.

A description should include:

- ✓ A clear topic
- ✓ Information that is organized in paragraphs
- ✓ Sensory details that paint a picture in the reader's mind
- ✓ Precise language and word choices that describe the topic

Read the prompt.

> Choose an event or a place and write a descriptive text about it. Your writing should be organized in paragraphs and should include sensory details and precise word choices that help readers imagine the topic you are writing about.

Plan Your Writing

Before you begin writing, brainstorm ideas. You can write about any place or event that interests you. Use your senses to think about sights, sounds, feelings, or smells. A web graphic organizer can help you develop your ideas. Write the name of your topic in the center oval. Then write sensory details that describe it in the outer ovals.

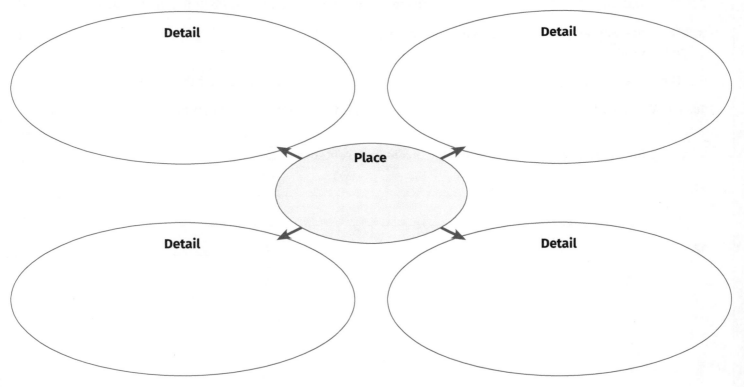

Write Your Descriptive Text

On the lines below or on a computer, write your descriptive text.

TIP
Write a first sentence that captures the reader's attention.

_____

_____

_____

_____

_____

_____

_____

_____

_____

Review Your Writing

Use this list to check your writing.

For practice with run-on sentences, complete the Language Skills Mini-Lesson on page 141.

- ☐ I focused on describing one topic.
- ☐ I used paragraphs to organize information.
- ☐ I used sensory details and precise language to make a picture in the reader's mind.
- ☐ I checked my spelling.
- ☐ I wrote complete, correct sentences.

After you check your work, make any corrections. Read your descriptive text aloud to a partner. Listen to your partner's text. Discuss what you pictured in your mind.

Think and Discuss

In 1897, three days after he was rescued, Stephen Crane published a newspaper report about the sinking of the SS Commodore. It was front page news and was titled "Stephen Crane's Own Story." It focuses mainly on the sinking of the ship and only two paragraphs are about the men on the dinghy. Read this adapted excerpt.

Less than two miles from Jacksonville, the terrible fog caused the pilot to ram the bow hard upon the mud. . . . the chief engineer cried hurriedly to the captain that there was something wrong in the engine room. A crew member turned to me and said: "Go help in the fireroom. They are going to bail with buckets." There was soapish sea water swirling and sweeping and swirling among machinery that roared and banged and clattered and steamed. Billy Higgins was sloshing around this inferno filling buckets with water and passing them to a chain of men.

How is the newspaper article different from and similar to the story "The Open Boat"? What do you visualize? How does this article sound different from a news article today? Discuss the questions in small groups.

The Last Leaf

In this lesson, you will

READ

the short story
- "The Last Leaf," by O Henry

USE THIS READING SKILL

Understand characters

USE THIS VOCABULARY SKILL

Understand words with the prefix *non-*

USE THIS WRITING SKILL

Write a character analysis

USE THESE KEY VOCABULARY WORDS

dreadful very bad; terrible

dreary dull and uninteresting, sad and gray

lantern a light inside a container with a handle for holding or hanging it

masterpiece a work of art, a piece of music, writing, etc. of the highest quality

nonsense words or actions that are foolish or untrue

persistent not stopping or going away

pneumonia an illness that affects your lungs and makes it difficult to breathe

pulp a soft, wet substance

scarcely almost not at all

twilight the period of the evening when there is a soft glowing light from the sky, between daylight and darkness

UNDERSTAND THESE CONTENT VOCABULARY WORDS

characters the people or animals in a story

make inferences to draw conclusions based on evidence and details

traits the adjectives that describe what a character is like

Marie Denise Villers, Oil on Canvas. Image courtesy of the The Metropolitan Museum of Art, Mr. and Mrs. Isaac D. Fletcher Collection, Bequest of Isaac D. Fletcher, 1917

Use the Vocabulary

Answer these questions about the vocabulary words. Use the definitions on page 114 to help you.

1. When would it be convenient to have a **lantern** with you?

   _____

2. What advice would you give to someone who has **pneumonia**?

   _____

3. What is your ideal way to spend a **dreary** Sunday afternoon?

   _____

4. Name two things that you think are **nonsense**.

   _____

5. If you could create a **masterpiece**, what would it be? Explain your answer.

   _____

6. What is the most **dreadful** weather you have been in or heard about?

   _____

7. What are you usually doing at **twilight**?

   _____

8. What should you do if you have a **persistent** cough?

   _____

9. Name something you do well now that you could **scarcely** do five years ago.

   _____

10. Do you like juice with or without **pulp**? Explain your answer.

   _____

VOCABULARY TIP

Some words have more than one meaning. To figure out the correct meaning of the word, look for clues in the text.

Read these sentences and look for clues about the meaning of *pulp*.

*When cardboard boxes are recycled, they are turned into **pulp** and made into newspapers.*

1. Which definition of pulp matches how the word is used in the sentence?
   a. *(noun)* the inner, juicy part of a fruit or vegetable
   b. *(noun)* a soft, wet substance made by crushing something like grain
   c. *(noun)* a soft material that is made mostly from wood and is used in making paper
   d. *(noun)* the substance that is left after the liquid has been squeezed from a fruit or vegetable

2. What clues helped you figure out the meaning? _____

Set a Purpose for Reading

Before reading, it helps to establish a purpose. The purpose is what you want to accomplish by the end of the reading. You can establish a purpose by asking yourself questions about what you are going to read. Look at the second paragraph of "The Last Leaf."

1. Who are the main characters? _____

2. What is the main problem in the story? _____

3. What do you want to know by the end of the story? _____

Take Notes

As you read, make notes in the margin. Underline important details in the text. This can help you pay attention as you read and find information later.

As you read, take notes. Use the prompts in the margin as you read.

Adapted from "The Last Leaf"
by O. Henry

1   Johnsy had **pneumonia**. She was very sick. She lay on her bed, looking through the window at the side of the house next door.

Make a note about what the doctor says about Johnsy.

2   The doctor told Sue, "Your roommate has a chance, but only if she wants to live. She has made up her mind that she's not going to get well. I will do what I can," he said. "But if she doesn't want to live, medicine is powerless."

3   After the doctor left, Sue cried a napkin into a **pulp**. Then she walked into Johnsy's room.

4   Johnsy lay facing the window. Her eyes were open wide. She was counting backward. "Nine," she said, and a little later "eight," and then "seven," and "six" almost together.

5   Sue looked out the window. What was there to count? There was only a **dreary** yard and the side of the brick house. An old vine climbed halfway up the wall. The cold winds of autumn had left its branches almost bare.

Make a note about Behrman's masterpiece.

6   "There are only five left, "Johnsy whispered.

7   "Five what?"

Make a note about why Johnsy is counting the leaves.

8   "Leaves. On the vine. When the last one falls I must go, too. Didn't the doctor tell you?"

9   "Oh, I never heard of such **nonsense**," answered Sue. "What do leaves have to do with your getting well? Try to have some soup now."

10 "No, I don't want anything," said Johnsy, her eyes fixed out the window. "There goes another. That leaves just four. I want to see the last one fall. Then I'll go, too."

11 "Johnsy," said Sue, "try to sleep. I'll pull the blind down so you stop looking at those leaves."

12 "I just want to see the last one fall," said Johnsy, closing her eyes, and lying white and still, "I'm tired of waiting. I'm tired of thinking."

13 "I have to go down and ask Behrman up to be my model. I won't be gone a minute," said Sue.

14 Behrman was a painter who lived on the ground floor. He was past sixty and never successful in art. He had always been about to paint a **masterpiece**, but had never begun it. For the past few years he had painted nothing. He earned a little money by modeling for artists. He still talked of his masterpiece.

15 Sue found Behrman in his apartment below. He had been drinking. Sue told him that Johnsy was very ill, and that the fever had left her mind full of strange ideas.

Check Your Comprehension

Answer these questions about the story.

1. What is Johnsy counting? _____

2. Who is Sue? _____

3. Who is Behrman? _____

Analyze Characters

The characters are the people in a story. You can make inferences about the characters from the way they look and the things that they think, say, and do. You can infer a character trait from something a character says or does only once or from a series of things the character does.

Answer these questions about the characters in the story.

1. In paragraph 2, what do you learn about how Johnsy feels about getting better?

   _____

2. What do you know about how Sue feels after talking to the doctor in paragraph 3?

   _____

3. What words in paragraph 8 tell you about Johnsy's attitude?

   _____

4. In contrast, how does Sue feel about Johnsy's plan? Look for clues in paragraph 9.

   _____

5. In paragraph 13, what does Sue say that implies she doesn't want to leave Johnsy alone too long?

   _____

6. Based on the information in paragraphs 14 and 15, what do you know about Behrman's life?

   _____

 IMPROVE YOUR READING

Practice reading paragraphs 6 through 13 of "The Last Leaf" silently. Pay attention to your expression, saying the quotes the way the characters would speak. With a partner, take turns reading the dialogue aloud.

Practice the Skills

Set a purpose for reading. Skim the text. Answer the questions.

1. What do the photo and the title have in common? _____

2. What has the weather been like? _____

3. What do you think will happen to Johnsy? _____

Read the article. As you read, use the prompts in the margin to help you make personal connections to the text.

Adapted from "The Last Leaf"

by O. Henry

Make a note about what Sue and Behrman did when they got upstairs.

1   Johnsy was sleeping when Sue and Behrman got upstairs. They looked out the window fearfully at the vine. Then they looked at each other for a moment without speaking. A cold rain was falling, mixed with snow. Behrman took his seat, and Sue began to paint.

2   When Sue awoke the next morning, after an hour's sleep, she found Johnsy staring at the closed shade. "Pull it up; I want to see," she whispered. She was **scarcely** moving.

Make a note about what didn't happen during the storm.

3   After the beating rain and strong winds that had lasted through the night, there was still one leaf against the brick wall. Still dark green, with yellow edges, it hung from the branch, 20 feet above the ground.

4   "It's the last one," said Johnsy. "I thought it would fall last night. I heard the wind. It will fall today, and I shall die."

5   The day passed, and even through the **twilight** they could see the lone leaf against the wall. At night the wind blew once more, while a **persistent** rain beat against the windows.

6   When it was light enough Johnsy asked Sue to raise the shade. The leaf was still there. Johnsy lay for a long time looking at it.

7   Then she called to Sue. "Something has made that last leaf stay there to show me that it is wrong to want to die. Bring a me a little soup. And help me sit up."

8   A little later she said, "Sue, some day I hope to paint in Italy."

Make a note about what new information the doctor shared with Sue.

9   The doctor came in the afternoon. "She'll be fine now, "he said, taking Sue's thin, shaking hand. And now I must see another case downstairs. Behrman—some kind of artist. Pneumonia, too. He is an old, weak man. There is no hope."

10 The next day afternoon Sue sat by Johnsy's bed. "I have something to tell you," she said. "Mr. Behrman died of pneumonia today. He was ill only two days. The janitor found him in his room downstairs. His shoes and clothing were wet and icy cold. They couldn't imagine where he had been on such a **dreadful** night. And then they found a **lantern**, still lighted, and a ladder, and some brushes, and green and yellow paint, and—look out the window at the last leaf on the wall. Didn't you wonder why it never moved when the wind blew? It's Behrman's masterpiece—he painted it there the night that the last leaf fell."

Check Your Comprehension

Answer these questions about the article.

1. Why did Sue sleep for only an hour? _____

_____

2. How did Johnsy's attitude change when she sees the last leaf still on the vine? _____

_____

3. How did Behrman save Johnsy's life? _____

_____

Practice Analyzing the Characters

One way to think about character traits is to use a graphic organizer. Write down what different characters say and do. Then list the character traits that match. Move back and forth between the columns.

HINT
The writer *implies*, or gives clues, about the characters. The reader *infers*, or draws conclusions, from the clues.

Fill in details about Johnsy, Sue, and Berhman in the chart. Use the details to draw a conclusion about each character.

	WHAT THE CHARACTER SAYS	WHAT THE CHARACTER DOES	WHAT YOU CAN INFER
Johnsy	1.	2.	3.
Sue	4.	5.	6.
Behrman	(no information)	7.	8.

 IMPROVE YOUR READING

Read paragraphs 9 and 10 of "The Last Leaf" silently. As you read, focus on grouping words together in phrases. Work with a partner. Take turns reading the paragraphs aloud.

Respond to the Readings

Answer these questions about the articles.

1. What does the doctor tell Sue about Johnsy's state of mind? _____

_____

2. "Oh, I never heard of such nonsense," answered Sue. What nonsense was Sue talking about?

_____

3. Why does Sue ask Behrman to come up to the apartment? _____

_____

4. How do you know that Johnsy decided she was going to get better? _____

_____

Use Word Parts: Prefix *non-*

The prefix *non-* means "not." You can add *non-* to the beginning of a noun, verb, adjective, or adverb to show the absence of something. For example, when you add the prefix *non-* to the noun *fat*, the new word is *nonfat*. There is no fat in nonfat milk.

Match the words on the left with the definitions on the right. Use a dictionary if you don't know the meaning of a word.

> **TIP**
> Writers often keep the hyphen when they add *non-* to a word that begins with *n*, as in *non-native*.

1. _____ noncommittal

a. difficult or impossible to burn

2. _____ nondairy

b. not done for the purpose of making money

3. _____ nondescript

c. something that does not make sense

4. _____ nonexistent

d. always going

5. _____ nonfiction

e. someone who doesn't live permanently in a particular place or country

6. _____ nonflammable

f. containing no milk or milk products

7. _____ nonprofit

g. appearing dull and not interesting or attractive

8. _____ nonresident

h. not existing at all

9. _____ nonsense

i. articles, books, etc. that are about real facts and events

10. _____ nonstop

j. not expressing a clear opinion or decision

Complete each sentence with a word from above.

11. When Zach feels nervous, he talks _____. It's like he never takes a breath.

12. For their safety, children's sleepwear should be _____.

13. The post office is in a small _____ building on Sixth Street. It's hard to find.

14. Helen works for a _____ organization that helps veterans.

Review the Vocabulary

Circle the letter of the answer that best completes each sentence.

1. If you need a **lantern**, _____.
   a. the power might be out
   b. it might be raining
   c. you might feel sleepy

2. If it is **dreary** out, the sky is probably _____.
   a. blue
   b. sunny
   c. dark

3. If you created a **masterpiece**, you would probably feel _____.
   a. proud
   b. sad
   c. sorry

4. If you worked past **twilight**, it was probably time for _____.
   a. breakfast
   b. lunch
   c. dinner

Complete each sentence with a word from the box.

dreadful	dreary	lantern	masterpiece	nonsense
persistent	pneumonia	pulp	scarcely	twilight

5. The reporter was _____. She kept asking questions until she got the answers she was looking for.

6. Some people think that astrology is just _____ and that there is no connection between who you are and when you were born.

7. Kenny was so tired, he could _____ keep his eyes open.

8. Lynn had double _____. Both her lungs are affected.

9. The house was in _____ condition after the party.

10. By the time I picked the report out of the puddle, it had already become a dirty wet _____.

Write two new sentences. Use a word from the box in each sentence.

11. _____

_____

12. _____

_____

Write a Character Analysis

When you read literature, you can analyze characters. You get to know characters through the things they say, feel, and do in the text. When you write a character analysis, you make inferences about the characters based on the evidence and details.

A character analysis should include:

- ✓ A sentence that tells your opinion of the character
- ✓ Reasons that support your opinion of the character
- ✓ Details and evidence about the character from the story
- ✓ Words and phrases that connect your opinion and reasons, such as *for example*, *because*, and *since*

Read the prompt.

> Write a character analysis of either Johnsy, Sue, or Behrman in "The Last Leaf." State your opinion of the character. Support your opinion with reasons. Include details and evidence from the story.

Plan Your Writing

Before you begin writing, review "The Last Leaf." Collect information about the character you chose and write it in the graphic organizer. Use the notes in the graphic organizer to develop your ideas.

Use the graphic organizer to think about your topic and take notes about what you will write.

CHARACTER

WHAT THE CHARACTER SAYS

WHAT THE CHARACTER DOES

WHAT YOU CAN INFER

Write Your Character Analysis

On the lines below or on a computer, write your character analysis.

TIP
If you are using exact words from the story or the exact words a character says, use quotation marks.

_____

_____

_____

_____

_____

_____

_____

_____

_____

Review Your Writing

Use this list to check your writing.

- ☐ I stated an opinion about a character.
- ☐ I gave reasons for my opinion.
- ☐ I used details and evidence from the story.
- ☐ I used words to connect ideas.
- ☐ I checked my punctuation and spelling
- ☐ I checked my punctuation.

For practice with commas and quotation marks, complete the Language Skills Mini-Lesson on page 142.

After you check your work, make any corrections. Read your text aloud to a partner. Then discuss how your texts were the same or different.

Think and Discuss

At the end of "The Last Leaf," Behrman risked his own life to save Johnsy's life. Talk about Behrman's decision. Would you risk your life to save another person?

iStock.com/mrtom-uk

Folktales

In this lesson, you will

READ
two folktales from different places:
- "Zomo the Rabbit," from West Africa
- "The Magpie and the Fox," from Korea

USE THIS READING SKILL
Understand a story's theme

USE THIS VOCABULARY SKILL
Understand words with the prefix *en-*

USE THIS WRITING SKILL
Write a comparison

USE THESE KEY VOCABULARY WORDS
caution care to avoid risks

clever smart

devise to think up or plan

devour to eat quickly or hungrily

entice to attract or lure

evade to stay away from; to avoid doing something

implement to put something into action

refuse to say no to a request

resist to keep yourself from doing something you want to do

wisdom knowledge gained through experience

UNDERSTAND THESE CONTENT VOCABULARY WORDS
plot the events that make up a story

theme an author's message or the central idea in a story

Use the Vocabulary

Answer these questions about the vocabulary words. Use the definitions on page 124 to help you.

1. Name a **clever** person you know. Why do you think that person is **clever**?

   _____

2. What are some things that might **entice** you to go outdoors? Why?

   _____

3. Describe a time when you **refused** to do something a boss, teacher, or someone else asked you to do. What happened next?

   _____

4. If you had to **devise** a plan for your future, what would it be?

   _____

5. Name a food that is difficult for you to **resist**. Why is it hard to **resist**?

   _____

6. Describe a time you **devoured** food. Explain why you **devoured** it.

   _____

7. When a company **implemented** a new computer program, the boss said, "Things will probably get worse before they get better." Why do you think she said that?

   _____

8. What are some ways an animal might **evade** a predator, or an animal that hunts it?

   _____

9. When are you most likely to use **caution**? Why are you cautious?

   _____

10. Tell about an experience that helped you gain **wisdom**.

   _____

VOCABULARY TIP

To figure out the meaning of a word you don't know, look for clues in the surrounding sentences. An author might give details that help you understand the word.

Read these sentences. Look for clues that help you figure out the meaning of *devour*. Then answer the questions.

*Great white sharks can **devour** large fish in seconds. They use rows of razor-sharp teeth to tear the fish into bite-sized pieces. Then they gulp it down.*

1. What are the details that help you understand the word *devour*? _____

2. Based on the details, what does *devour* mean? _____

Set a Purpose for Reading

Before you read the story, think about what you want to find out. Start by looking at the title. Skim the selection. Then look at the questions on page 127.

1. From the title, what do you think this story will be about? _____

2. Based on what you know about folktales, what do you expect from this story? _____

3. Preview the questions on page 127. What should you pay attention to as you read? _____

Predict

As you read, think about the story's characters. Based on what they have done, predict what they will do next.

Read the passage. As you read, make predictions. Answer the questions in the margin.

"Zomo the Rabbit"
A West African Folktale

1 Zomo the Rabbit was not big or strong, but he was quite fast. He was also **clever**, but he thought it would be better to be wise. He decided to ask Sky God for **wisdom**. "Please, Sky God, please give me wisdom."

2 Sky God laughed and said, "Wisdom must always be *earned*, Zomo. You can earn wisdom if you complete three tasks, though they may be impossible: you must get scales from Big Fish, milk from Wild Cow, and a tooth from Leopard."

> Do you think Zomo will accomplish the tasks listed in paragraph 2?

3 Zomo believed he could accomplish the tasks because he was fast and clever. Zomo **devised** a plan.

4 He played his drums at the edge of the sea, knowing Big Fish could not **resist** coming out of the water to dance. When Big Fish appeared, Zomo played faster and louder. This made Big Fish dance so fast and so hard that his scales shook loose and fell to the ground. Naked and embarrassed, he ran back into the sea.

5 Zomo scooped up the scales and began his next "impossible" task. He climbed a tree near Wild Cow and started teasing her. He pointed, laughed, and called her weak. Enraged, Wild Cow charged at Zomo, causing her horns to get stuck in the tree. While Wild Cow was stuck, Zomo climbed down and milked her.

> What do you think Zomo will do after he gets the scales from Big Fish?

6 Next, Zomo hopped up the mountain where Leopard lived. He used the scales from Big Fish and the milk from Wild Cow to make a slippery mess on the path. Leopard came along, slipped in the mess, and tumbled down the rocky slope. Zomo rushed to Leopard, who sat on the ground, holding one of his big, sharp teeth in his paw. Zomo grabbed the tooth and dashed away quickly before Leopard could eat him.

7 Zomo looked to the sky. "I did it, Sky God! I accomplished everything you asked."

> Predict what will happen when Sky God finds out Zomo was successful.

8 "Very well, Zomo. I will tell you the secret to wisdom. To have wisdom, you must have courage, and you were very courageous today. You must also have good sense, and you used some good sense today. Last, you must have **caution**. But Zomo, today you were not at all cautious. When you are cautious, as well as being courageous and sensible, only then will you have wisdom."

9 The next time Zomo faced a dangerous situation, he used caution and ran to safety. That is when Zomo the rabbit realized he was not only fast and clever. He was also wise.

Check Your Comprehension

Answer these questions about the folktale.

1. Who are the characters in the story? _____

2. What does Zomo the Rabbit want Sky God to give him? _____

3. What three tasks does Sky God tell Zomo he must complete? _____

_____

Understand a Story's Theme

A story's theme is its message or lesson. If a story's lesson is not obvious or directly stated, think about the plot (the story's events), along with how and why the characters change. Look for lessons the characters learn.

Answer these questions about the folktale to find its theme.

1. What problem does Zomo have at the beginning of the story? _____

_____

2. Zomo the Rabbit is fast and clever. Which of these traits does Zomo use to get scales from Big Fish? What does this tell you about Zomo?

_____

3. Which traits—speed, cleverness, or both—does Zomo use to get a tooth from Leopard? What does this tell you about Zomo?

_____

4. After Zomo completes the tasks, why doesn't Sky God give him wisdom? _____

_____

5. At the end of the story, Zomo knows he is wise. How does he know? _____

_____

6. Do you agree that Zomo gained wisdom in this story? Explain. _____

_____

7. Which sentence best tells the theme of this folktale?

   a. It is more important to be fast than to be strong.

   b. To become wise, you must use courage, good sense, and caution.

   c. If you are not cautious, you had better be fast.

 IMPROVE YOUR READING

Practice reading paragraph 4 of "Zomo the Rabbit" silently. Then listen while your teacher reads it aloud. Pay attention to your teacher's pace, or the speed. Next, read the paragraph aloud with your teacher, paying attention to pace.

Practice the Skills

Set a purpose before you begin reading. Answer the questions.

1. Read the title. What will the story be about? _____

2. Read the questions on page 129. What should you look for as you read? _____

3. What do you want to learn about the characters in this story? _____

As you read, make predictions. Answer the questions in the margin.

TIP
A *magpie* is a common bird that is known for having a loud voice.

"The Magpie and the Fox"
A Korean Folktale

Do you think the fox will get a magpie chick?

TIP
A *quail* is a bird often eaten for food. A *stork* is sometimes a symbol of good luck and long life.

1 One day, a fox passed under a magpie's nest, where the magpie was raising her young. Upon seeing the chicks, the fox asked to have one for his breakfast. The magpie **refused**, of course.

2 "If you don't," the fox said, "I will climb up and take them all."

3 The magpie was so frightened she threw down a chick, which the fox quickly **devoured**. Sadly, the same thing happened again the next day.

Watercolor by Rachel Toll for The Fox and the Magpie, used by permission of the artist.

4 When the quail (a clever bird) overheard the conversation, she decided to have a talk with the magpie. "Don't be foolish, Mrs. Magpie," the quail said. "The fox cannot climb a tree." The next day, the magpie refused to give the fox a chick, instead telling him what the quail had said.

5 The fox was very annoyed and complained to the quail until she agreed to provide him with a meal. Being a clever bird, she found a woman who was walking through the forest carrying a bowl of rice for some nearby workers. The woman thought the quail would make a tasty dinner, so she began to chase it. The quail went faster, **enticing** the woman deeper into the forest.

What do you think happens after the quail feeds the fox on the third day?

6 Finally the woman put down the rice so she could run faster and have her hands free to grab the quail. The quail kept going deeper into the forest, and the woman was not far behind. When the woman and the rice were long separated, the quail flew to the fox and told him where to find the bowl of rice. This happened for three days in a row.

7 The quail grew tired of working so hard to feed the fox, so she went to see the stork (a very wise bird) to get some advice. After hearing how the fox had tricked Mrs. Magpie and taken advantage of the quail's kindness, the stork said the quail had enough reason to kill the fox.

Do you think the quail will manage to kill the fox?

8 The quail created a plan to do just that. She would solve the problem with the fox once and for all.

9 When the quail saw a man trapping birds, she began to **implement** her plan. "Mr. Fox, there is a hunter in the forest. You should hide under this grass." The quail helped the fox hide beneath a pile of grass. Then she went off to find the hunter.

TIP
The word *lame* means "unable to walk well because of an injury."

10 To make the hunter think she was lame, the quail limped and fluttered. When he drew back his arm to hit her with a stick, she **evaded** him, and he broke his trap. Being angry, the hunter drew back again, just as the quail landed on the grass that was covering the fox. As the hunter swung down, the quail moved out of the way. The hunter hit—and killed—the troublesome fox.

Check Your Comprehension

Answer these questions about the folktale.

1. Who are the main characters in this folktale? _____

2. What does the fox make the magpie do? _____

3. How does the quail help the magpie? _____

Practice Understanding a Story's Theme

The theme of a story is its main message or lesson. Sometimes a story's theme or lesson is obvious, but usually readers have to find the theme using clues from the story. An important clue can be a character who learns a lesson, such as when a character is rewarded for good behavior or punished for bad behavior. The lesson learned by the character is often the story's theme or main message.

Complete the graphic organizer by answering each question.

Who are the main characters?
1.

↓

What problem or conflict do the characters face?
2.

↓

What do the characters do about the problem?
3.

↓

What happens to the characters? Is anyone rewarded or punished?
4.

↓

What lesson do the characters learn? What is the story's theme?
5.

 IMPROVE YOUR READING

Practice reading paragraph 4 of "The Magpie and the Fox" silently. Pay attention to the parentheses, which surround information that is less important than the rest of the sentence. Say the words in quotation marks the same way the character might say them. Next, listen to your teacher read the paragraph aloud, noticing how your teacher's voice changes at the parentheses and quotation marks. Then read the paragraph aloud with your teacher.

Respond to the Readings

Answer these questions about the folktales.

1. In "Zomo the Rabbit," why do you think Sky God call the tasks "impossible"? _____

_____

2. What do you think Zomo did in the story that made Sky God say he was not cautious? _____

_____

3. In "The Magpie and the Fox," how does the quail solve the problem? _____

_____

4. Do you think the magpie learned anything by the end of the story? Explain. _____

_____

5. Which character from "The Magpie and the Fox" is most like the character of Zomo? In what ways are the two characters similar?

_____

Use Word Parts: Prefix *en–*

By knowing the meaning of word parts, including prefixes, suffixes, and roots, readers can often determine the meaning of unfamiliar words. The prefix *en-* means "in." For example, to *enslave* someone means to put into slavery. To *enrage* someone means to cause rage in them.

Read each sentence. Use context clues, your knowledge of word parts, or a dictionary to write the meaning of the underlined word.

1. The woman <u>encircled</u> her trees with mulch and decorative stones.

_____

2. When you mail in your order, please <u>enclose</u> a check for the full amount owed.

_____

3. Computers <u>encode</u> information using only ones and zeros.

_____

4. At the museum, all the ancient pots and other artifacts are <u>encased</u> in glass so that nobody touches them.

_____

5. The mountain gorilla is one of the most <u>endangered</u> animals on the planet. There are fewer than 1,000 of them.

_____

6. Can you <u>envision</u> a world in which robots do all your household chores?

_____

TIP
Watch out for prefix lookalikes. For example, the word *environment* seems to use the prefix *en-*, but *en* is actually part of the word's root, *environ*. Likewise, the word *endless* does not have a prefix. *En* is part of the word's root, *end*.

Review the Vocabulary

Read each group of words. Write the vocabulary word from the box that best goes with each group of words.

caution	clever	devise	devour	entice
evade	implement	refuse	resist	wisdom

1. avoid, sidestep, dodge _____

2. say no to, reject, deny _____

3. lure, attract, bait _____

4. gobble, consume, eat with greed _____

5. carefulness, avoidance of risk, attention _____

Complete each sentence with a word from the box.

6. Before we _____ a travel plan, we need to request time off work.

7. I try to _____ taking a piece of candy from the bowl on my boss's desk, but it's my favorite kind.

8. Knowledge can come from a book, but _____ only comes from experience.

9. My cat is so _____ that he can open the cabinet door and get to his treats.

10. The boss said, "These are the new rules for salespeople. I'd like you to _____ them immediately."

Write two new sentences. Use a word from the box in each sentence.

11. _____

_____

12. _____

_____

Write a Comparison

We make comparisons all the time. For example, you might compare a movie to the book that it is based on. You might compare two professional sports teams to figure which one will probably win a game. When you're shopping, you might compare two different pairs of shoes by looking at their color, style, and price before you choose the pair you will buy. You can also compare characters in different stories. When you compare characters, you can think about ways they are alike and different, what kind of problems they face, and what kind of lessons they learn.

A comparison should include:

- ✓ An introductory sentence telling whether the characters are mostly the same or mostly different
- ✓ A paragraph telling important ways the characters are the same
- ✓ A paragraph telling important ways the characters are different
- ✓ Linking words that show connections between ideas
- ✓ A conclusion summarizing your ideas about the two characters

Read the prompt.

> Write a comparison of Zomo in "Zomo the Rabbit" and the quail in "The Magpie and the Fox." Be sure to tell how the two characters are the same and different.

Plan Your Writing

Before you begin writing, plan your comparison. Use the graphic organizer to take notes about the main similarities and differences between the two characters. Then use the information to write your comparison.

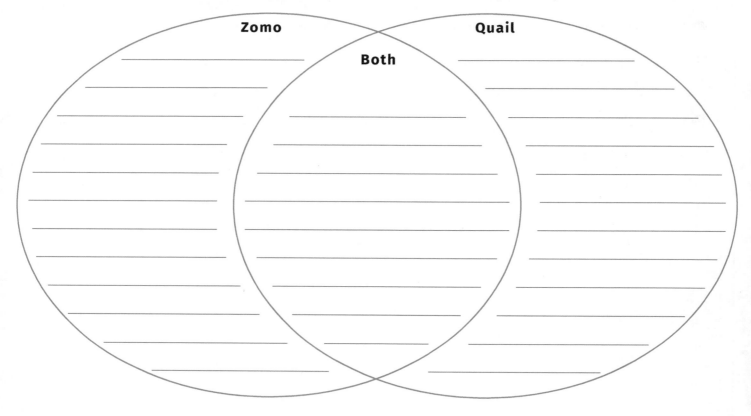

Write Your Comparison

On the lines below or on a computer, write your comparison.

TIP

Use one paragraph to tell similarities and another paragraph to tell differences.

_____

_____

_____

_____

_____

_____

_____

_____

_____

_____

Review Your Writing

Use this list to check your writing.

- ☐ I told what two characters I am comparing.
- ☐ I told how the characters are alike.
- ☐ I told how the characters are different.
- ☐ I checked my spelling and punctuation.
- ☐ I wrote complete sentences.

After you check your work, make any corrections. Read your comparison aloud to a partner. Listen to your partner's comparison. How are your comparisons alike and different? Discuss the reasons for any differences.

Think and Discuss

The character Zomo is what's known as a "trickster" figure. Tricksters are smart. They use their cleverness to get what they want, to play tricks, or to break common rules.

Think of a trickster character in a story you know, such as a fable, a TV cartoon, or a movie. Discuss these questions about the tricksters you identified.

- What does the trickster do to others?

- How do other characters react to the trickster's behavior?

- How is the trickster rewarded or punished?

Renard the Fox by Michel Rodange (1869) Ernest Griset Illustrator (PD–US)

Read the article. Circle the best answer to each question.

Adapted from
Rebecca of Sunnybrook Farm
by Kate Douglas Wiggin

1   "Your farm ain't the old Hobbs place, is it?" Mr. Cobb asked his young passenger.

2   "No, it's just Randall's Farm. At least that's what mother calls it. I call it Sunnybrook Farm."

3   "I guess it don't make no difference what you call it so long as you know where it is," remarked Mr. Cobb.

4   Rebecca turned the full light of her eyes upon him almost severely, as she answered, "Oh! Don't say that, and be like all the rest! It does make a difference what you call things. When I say Randall's Farm, do you see how it looks?"

5   "No, I can't say I do," responded Mr. Cobb uneasily.

6   "Now when I say Sunnybrook Farm, what does it make you think of?"

7   Mr. Cobb felt like a fish removed from his native elements and left panting on the sand. There was no avoiding the awful responsibility of a reply, for Rebecca's eyes were searchlights.

8   "I suppose there's a brook somewhere near it," he said.

9   Rebecca looked disappointed but not quite disheartened. "That's pretty good," she said encouragingly. "There's a brook, but not a common brook. It has young trees and baby bushes on each side of it, and it's a shallow little brook with a white sandy bottom and lots of little shiny pebbles. Whenever there's a bit of sunshine the brook catches it, and it's always full of sparkles the livelong day."

Rebecca of Sunnybrook Farm (1931) by Kate Douglass. Helen Mason Grose Illustrator.

10   After a pause, she added, "I wish I could see Milltown. I suppose it's big and grand like Paris?"

11   "Paris ain't so great," said Mr. Cobb. "It's the dullest place in the state of Maine. I've driven there many a time."

12   Rebecca was quick to correct Mr. Cobb.

13   "Paris is the capital of France, and you have to go to it on a boat," she explained. "It's in my geography book, and it says: 'The French are a gay and polite people, fond of dancing and light wines.' I can see Paris as plain as day by just shutting my eyes. The beautiful ladies are always gayly dancing around, and the grand gentlemen are politely dancing and drinking light wines. But you can see Milltown most every day with your eyes wide open," Rebecca said wistfully.

---

1. Which word below best describes Rebecca?

   a. honest

   b. reliable

   c. kind

   d. imaginative

2. In paragraph 7, what is the author telling us when she writes that "Mr. Cobb felt like a fish removed from his native elements"?

   a. He is uncomfortable answering Rebecca's question.

   b. He doesn't know what Rebecca is talking about.

   c. He wants to stop and have lunch.

   d. He can't breathe and he thinks he is dying.

3. Based on paragraphs 12 and 13, what can you infer about Rebecca?

   a. She likes geography.

   b. She is self-confident.

   c. She is interested in dancing.

   d. She makes a lot of mistakes.

4. Why does the writer compare Rebecca's eyes to searchlights in paragraph 7?

   a. They are bright and large and round.

   b. They can move in different directions.

   c. They are glowing.

   d. They can find things that are hidden in the dark.

Sentence Fragments

A **sentence fragment** may look like a sentence, but it is incomplete and incorrect.

- A fragment does not tell a complete thought.
- It might be missing its subject (the naming part), its predicate (the telling part), or both.

Fragment: After he studied. (incomplete thought; what happened after he studied?)

Sentence: After he studied, he went for a run. (complete thought)

When a sentence is a **command**, it won't include a stated subject. The subject of a command is understood to be the word "you."

Command: Please wash the produce carefully.

Command: Before starting the test, turn off your phone.

Read each group of words. If it is a complete sentence, write *S*. If it is a sentence fragment, write *F*. Add words to each fragment to make a correct sentence.

TIP
You can't tell if a group of words is a fragment by looking at its length. A complete sentence can be very short, such as *We walked*, and a fragment can be long, such as *After we walked to the grocery store on Main Street.*

1. _____ Goes to work at the store at 10 p.m. and stays until 6 a.m.

   _____

2. _____ Fresh produce near the front of the store.

   _____

3. _____ Eggs and milk are usually at the back of the store.

   _____

4. _____ Before you shop, eat something.

   _____

5. _____ Fruits and vegetables, meat, fish, eggs, and dairy products.

   _____

6. _____ Spends a little over three minutes waiting to check out.

   _____

7. _____ Stores today give shoppers bigger shopping carts to get them to buy more.

   _____

8. _____ The samples of food that some stores give shoppers.

   _____

Frequently Confused Words

Frequently confused words look alike, sound alike, or look and sound alike but have different meanings.

Match the word with its definition. Write the correct letter on each line.

1. _____ accept   **a.** receive or take something willingly

      _____ except   **b.** not including someone or something

2. _____ advice   **a.** to recommend

      _____ advise   **b.** a recommendation

3. _____ affect   **a.** to cause a change

      _____ effect   **b.** a result

4. _____ already   **a.** by this time

      _____ all ready   **b.** prepared

5. _____ loose   **a.** to be unable to find something

      _____ lose   **b.** not tight

6. _____ maybe   **a.** perhaps

      _____ may be   **b.** might be

7. _____ weather   **a.** climate conditions

      _____ whether   **b.** if

8. _____ whose   **a.** *who* + *is* or *who* + *has*

      _____ who's   **b.** possessive form of *who*

Complete the sentences. Circle the correct word in parentheses.

9. Do you know (weather / whether) the flower shop accepts debit cards?

10. (Maybe / May be) Robert left his debit card at the coffee shop.

11. Jim took his friend's (advice / advise) and opened a bank account.

12. (Who's / Whose) decision was it to stay open late on Fridays?

13. Rita's positive experience had a big (affect / effect) on my decision to try yoga.

Capitalization

- Capitalize the names and titles of **people**.
  Mr. Scott Martin, Dr. Lola Garcia, Uncle Jim

- Capitalize the names of **places**, such as cities, states, countries, continents, streets, bodies or water, and monuments. Do not capitalize words like *the* or *of*.
  Gulf of Mexico, Harrisburg, Arizona, Spain, Africa, Oak Street

- Capitalize the names of **events**, **documents**, **nationalities**, and **languages**.
  World War I, the Constitution, Americans, Spanish

- Capitalize the first, last, and all important words in the **titles of works**.
  Fall of the House of Usher, The New York Times, The Wonderful Wizard of Oz

Write the words that should begin with a capital letter on the line.

1. ms. jane franklin _____

2. continent _____

3. europe _____

4. santa fe trail _____

5. the railroad _____

6. mississippi river _____

7. *call of the wild*, by jack london _____

TIP
Titles of longer works, such as books, movies, and films, are written in italics. Titles of shorter works, like poems, short stories, and articles, are placed inside quotation marks.

Rewrite the sentences with correct capitalization.

8. the book *little house on the prairie* was written by laura ingalls wilder.

_____

9. many soldiers who fought in the civil war got jobs with the union pacific railroad.

_____

10. the oregon trail went from independence, missouri, to oregon city, oregon.

_____

11. travelers stopped at fort Kearney and then followed the platte river.

_____

12. many chinese immigrants came to the united states during the california gold rush.

_____

13. marcus and narcissa whitman were missionaries who wanted to convert the cayuse indians.

_____

Shifts in Tense

Verb tenses tell you when an action takes place. A verb describes an action. Sentences often have more than one verb. When this is the case, the verb tenses should match if the actions take place during the same time period.

Incorrect: The government designed and creates thousands of posters.

Correct: The government designed and created thousands of posters during World War II.

Correct: The government designs and creates thousands of posters every year.

Read the sentences. If the sentence is correct as is, write *C*. If there is an inappropriate shift in tense, rewrite the sentence with correct verb tenses.

TIP
If a sentence is confusing to you, there's a good chance there's been a verb tense shift.

1. Millions of families <u>plant</u> Victory Gardens and <u>grew</u> their own vegetables.

   _____

2. Food rationing <u>began</u> in 1942 and <u>will continue</u> for a year after the war.

   _____

3. People <u>got</u> food ration books that limited what they <u>bought</u> and when.

   _____

4. Gas <u>was</u> rationed and so <u>were</u> tires and fuel.

   _____

5. Rationing books <u>have</u> deadlines for when you <u>could</u> use the stamps.

   _____

Complete each sentence with the verb in parentheses in the correct verb tense.

6. The Navajo language _____ (have) four vowels that _____ (be) either long or short.

7. Philip Johnston _____ (grow up) with the Navajo people and _____ (speak) the language fluently.

8. Johnston _____ (believe) that the code _____ (be) unbreakable, and the code talkers _____ (prove) that he _____ (be) right.

Circle the letter of the answer that best completes each sentence.

9. The Navajo Nation extends into the states of Utah, Arizona, and New Mexico, and _____ over 27,000 square miles.
   a. covered   b. will cover   c. covers

10. The Navajo Nation _____ a veteran's memorial to honor the Navajos who served in the U.S. military.
    a. built   b. will built   c. builds

Commas

Use a comma before a conjunction in a compound sentence.
> We can drive to class, or we can take the bus.
> My English class goes until 2 p.m., and I have to be at work at 2:30.

Use a comma to separate three or more elements in a series.
> Melissa grows tomatoes, peppers, and squash in her garden.
> She jogs, bikes, and swims to get ready for a race.

Use a comma after an introductory prepositional phrase or dependent clause.
> At the beginning of class, our teacher writes goals for the day on the board.
> After he reads the paper, Dan walks the dog.

Use a comma to set off all geographical names.
> We moved to Harrisburg, Pennsylvania, when I was five years old.
> I want to visit Vera Cruz, Mexico, next year.

Add commas to the sentences where they are needed. If no commas are needed, leave the sentence as is.

TIP
Elements in a series can be any part of speech, such as nouns, verbs, adjectives, and adverbs.

1. Because of censorship during the war newspapers were not allowed to report on flu outbreaks.

2. Bubonic plague first came to Europe at the port of Messina Sicily.

3. During the second wave of the flu there was an outbreak near Boston Massachusetts that soon spread to other places.

4. Doctors nurses and other medical workers became sick while treating flu patients.

5. In just a few years about one-third of the world's population died from bubonic plague.

6. The flu pandemic of 1918 killed 50 million to 100 million people.

7. The flu spread rapidly and people weren't sure how to stop it.

8. To stop the spread of the flu officials closed schools churches and theaters.

9. When soldiers were sent to fight in World War I they carried the flu with them.

10. Some of the symptoms of plague included black spots on skin fever vomiting and lumps.

11. Bubonic plague was caused by a kind of bacteria.

12. Past outbreaks of flu had killed mainly young old or sick people.

13. Some people died within hours of getting the first symptoms of the flu.

Conditionals

Conditional sentences have two clauses: a condition (*if . . .*) and a result.

	IF CLAUSE (CONDITION)	MAIN CLAUSE (RESULT)
Zero Conditional (Real)	If it rains,	I take my umbrella.
First Conditional (Future Real)	If it rains,	I will take my umbrella.
Second Conditional (Future Unreal)	If it rained,	I would take my umbrella.
Third Conditional (Past Unreal)	If it had rained,	I would have taken my umbrella.

Circle the letter of the answer that best completes each sentence.

1. If Ana _____, she will become a firefighter.

   a. wants

   b. will want

   c. wanted

   d. had wanted

2. Mudslides often _____ if there are bad wildfires in the hillsides of southern California.

   a. happen

   b. will happen

   c. happened

   d. had happened

3. Even if there _____ no wildfires, there would still be mudslides.

   a. are

   b. will be

   c. were

   d. had been

4. If Sara had lived in Texas during the Dust Bowl, she _____ her home to save her family.

   a. abandons

   b. will abandon

   c. abandoned

   d. would have abandoned

TIP

It isn't always clear if a single sentence is a real or a future real conditional. In a text, however, you can often find clues in the surrounding sentences.

Complete each sentence with the correct form of the verb in parentheses.

5. Lee won't leave the house if it (keep) on raining.

   _____

6. If Black Sunday hadn't happened, Woody Guthrie (write / not) "So Long It's Been Good to Know Yuh."

   _____

7. If we had the time, we (read) more about Woody Guthrie's life.

   _____

8. The 2018 mudslide would not have been so bad if the Thomas fire (be / not) so big.

   _____

9. People wore masks if the dust (blow) really hard

   _____

Run-On Sentences

A **run-on sentence** is two or more independent clauses (complete sentences) that are combined without correct punctuation.

> *Run-on sentence:* Rosa was cutting the grass Ron was watering the garden.

You can correct a run-on sentence by rewriting it as two complete sentences. Each sentence must have a subject, a verb, and end punctuation:

> *Corrected sentence:* Rosa was cutting the grass. Ron was watering the garden.

You can also correct a run-on sentence by adding a comma and a conjunction to join the parts of the sentence. The conjunctions *and*, *but*, *or*, *for*, *nor*, *yet*, and *so* can be used to join sentence parts.

> *Corrected sentence:* Rosa was cutting the grass, and Ron was watering the garden.

Read each sentence. If it is a run-on, correct it by writing it as two complete sentences. If it is correct, write *correct*.

TIP
You can't tell if a sentence is a run-on just by looking at its length. Think about whether it tells two complete ideas.

1. Tuesdays are the worst day to ride the bus it is very crowded.

   _____

2. The story describes what it is like to be on a tiny lifeboat at sea.

   _____

3. Marco drives to class he parks in the lot on First Street.

   _____

4. I can't use my cell phone the battery level is too low.

   _____

Read each sentence. If it is a run-on, correct it by adding a comma and a conjunction (and, but, or, for, nor, yet, so). If it is correct, write correct.

5. The test was very hard Linda got an A.

   _____

6. The room is small and dark Tina wants to paint it a bright color.

   _____

7. Fred will go to truck driving school he will sign up for college classes.

   _____

8. The basketball game was exciting the team made some amazing shots.

   _____

Commas and Quotation Marks

Direct quotations are the exact words that someone said or wrote. Direct quotations always go inside quotation marks.

Use a comma to introduce a quotation.
    Johnsy counted, "Eight."

Put commas inside quotation marks.
    "I will do what I can," the doctor said.

Indirect quotations tell what someone has said or written, but they don't use the exact words. Indirect quotations don't go inside quotation marks.
    Sue told Behrman that Johnsy was very ill.

TIP
These comma rules are for American English. If you see commas used differently, you may be reading something by a British writer.

Rewrite each sentence. Add commas in the correct place.

1. "If she were interested in the future, her chances would be better" said the doctor.

2. Sue answered "She always wanted to paint in Italy."

3. "I want to see the last leaf fall" explained Johnsy. "I have done enough waiting."

4. "I'm going to close the blind" said Sue. "I don't want you to look at those leaves."

5. "Try to sleep" whispered Sue. She closed the door behind her.

Rewrite each sentence. Add quotation marks and commas where they are needed. If no change is needed, write *correct*.

6. Behrman cried That poor little Johnsy!

7. She is very sick and weak said Sue.

8. Behrman replied Someday I will paint my masterpiece.

9. He shouted his anger over Johnsy's plan.

UNIT 1

LESSON 1

Vocabulary Tip, p. 9

1. c
2. Answers will vary.

Check Your Comprehension, p. 11

1. It is about how to shop for food at the grocery store.
2. The most expensive items are at eye level. Less expensive items are on the top and bottom shelves.
3. The diagram shows the layout of a grocery store.

Recall Key Details, p. 11

1. **a.** plan before you shop
   b. understand the store layout
2. Check your cabinets so that you don't buy something you already have at home.
3. Hungry shoppers buy things that aren't on their lists.
4. Bring cash to pay for groceries.
5. Healthy foods are set up on the perimeter of the store.
6. fresh fruits and vegetables, milk, eggs, meat, and fish
7. expensive items are placed at eye level on the shelves; endcap displays; stores place unneeded items at the registers
8. Shoppers spend 3 minutes 11 seconds in line. During that time, you can see and buy something you don't need.

Check Your Comprehension, p. 13

1. A community garden is a piece of land shared by a group of gardeners.
2. A community garden can improve health, the environment, and communities.
3. The first photo shows an empty lot with a lot of trash. The second photo shows a garden growing.

Practice Recalling Key Details, p. 13

1. Food deserts are communities without access to fresh, healthy food that people can afford.

2. 18 million Americans live in food deserts.
3. Gardeners and people who want fresh food can benefit from a community garden.
4. Produce travels an average of 1,500 miles.
5. It travels by trucks, trains, boats, and planes that pollute.
6. It takes 7 to 14 days to reach a store.
7. About half the food spoils.
8. To get food from a farm to your table, the food must travel long distances and long periods of times.
9. Food in a community garden doesn't have to travel far and it remains fresh.

Respond to the Readings, p. 14

1. Planning and understanding how a grocery store is set up can help you save money and make better choices when you shop.
2. Answers will vary.
3. Community gardens allow people to grow their own food, and benefit their health, the environment, and the community.
4. The first benefits would be people having fresh produce to eat and getting exercise. It would take longer to improve the environment and change the community.
5. *Possible responses:* Similar: Both articles discuss ways people get food and how people can get healthier food. Different: The first article discusses smart ways of shopping for all kinds of food, while the second article talks specifically about the benefits of growing your own produce.

Use Word Parts, p. 14

1. transfer
2. transplant
3. translate
4. transportation
5. transaction
6–7. Sentences will vary.

Review the Vocabulary, p. 15

1. a
2. a
3. c
4. b
5. budget
6. transformed
7. afford
8. display
9. access
10. transport
12–13. Sentences will vary.

LESSON 2

Vocabulary Tip, p. 19

answer

Check Your Comprehension, p. 21

1. Workers in the past found jobs in newspaper ads and help wanted signs in shop windows.
2. To find a job, workers can go to job search websites, networking websites, and community job centers.
3. Employers and workers both benefit from job search websites.

Identify Reasons and Evidence, p. 21

1. Strategies for finding a job have changed a lot from 25 years ago.
2. Workers used to find jobs in newspaper ads or from help wanted signs. Now they find jobs online.
3. The author says ads and help wanted signs were inefficient because it could take several weeks to get a response, and depended on being in the right place at the right time.
4. Online job hunting helps workers accomplish goals sooner. They can look at a lot of jobs, connect with a lot of people, and apply for jobs immediately.
5. Job search websites benefit employers.
6. Employers can reach a lot of people quickly and easily.
7. a, b

Check Your Comprehension, p. 23

1. Workers should consider other work opportunities.
2. The three main work opportunities discussed in the article are volunteering, internships, and part-time jobs.
3. Volunteering is unpaid work to help others.

Practice Identifying Reasons and Evidence, p. 23

1. People who can't find full-time work right away should stay busy by volunteering, interning, and working part-time.
2. Close the gap of unemployment on your resume or application
3. Network to build job connections
4. Build your job skills to stay current or learn new skills
5. Improve your mental health
6. Volunteering also helps the community, and it might give you the opportunity to explore a new line of work.
7. With an internship, you get the added benefit of gaining work experience and connections in your field, and you might get paid.
8. Answers will vary.

Respond to the Readings, p. 24

1. Job hunting was harder in the past because responding to want ads was inefficient and responding to help wanted signs required that a person be in the right place at the right time.
2. Answers will vary.
3. An internship is a job in your field; volunteer work and part-time work might be in your field, but not always. Volunteer work is not paid, sometimes internships are paid, and part-time work is always paid. An internship lasts for a certain period of time, but volunteering and part-time work can continue.
4. Answers will vary.
5. Answers will vary. Both articles give information about ways of finding work. The first article talks about ways to look for work, while the second article talks about work opportunities other than full-time work.

Use Word Parts, p. 24

1. conclude
2. consequences
3. conflict
4. consistent
5. contour

6–7. Answers will vary.

Review the Vocabulary, p. 25

1. c
2. b
3. c
4. c
5. respond
6. advantage
7. convince
8. profile
9. strategy
10. obvious

LESSON 3

Vocabulary Tip, p. 29

1. b
2. c
3. a

Check Your Comprehension, p. 31

1. Decision making is personal because you have to think about what's important to you.
2. You can talk to people who have had to make a similar decision. You can go online and learn as much as you can.
3. Answers will vary.

Understand Cause and Effect, p. 31

1. b

Possible answers:

2. There are no right answers because decision making is personal.
3. If you imagine the results of each option, you'll see that some options are more likely to help you reach your goal.
4. Research your options online, and consequently you will make a good decision.

5. Review your decision in order to make better decisions in the future.
6. You spent a long time making the decision, for that reason, act on it.

Check Your Comprehension, p. 33

1. Your credit limit is based on your credit history.
2. Your balance goes down.
3. You will be charged interest.

Practice Understanding Cause and Effect, p. 33

1. c
2. b
3. d
4. a

Possible answers:

5. You add to your balance *because* you make a purchase.
6. *If* you don't pay off your balance, you will be charged interest.
7. You pay a fee *as a result* of going over your credit limit.
8. You reduce your balance *when* you make a payment.

Graphic organizer effects:

there are no monthly fees, payments, or interest charges

you can only use as much money as you have in your account

if you use more money than you have, the bank will charge an overdraft fee

Respond to the Readings, p. 34

1. Answers will vary.
2. b
3. You may be charged a fee for cash advances, late payments, or for going over your limit.
4. You can spend only as much money as you have. There is no credit involved.
5. Answers will vary.

Use Word Parts, p. 34

1. artistic
2. athletic
3. basic
4. economic

5. electronic
6. historic
7. economic
8. electronic
9. basic
10. angelic
11. scenic
12. patriotic

Review the Vocabulary, p. 35

1. a
2. c
3. b
4. c
5. loan
6. borrow
7. Appropriate
8. specific
9. adjust
10. transfer

Unit 1 Review, p. 38

1. d
2. a
3. b
4. c

UNIT 2

LESSON 4

Vocabulary Tip, p. 41

d

Check Your Comprehension, p. 43

1. It started in Independence, Missouri, and ended in Oregon City, Oregon.
2. The trip was long, the work was exhausting, and the conditions were difficult.
3. Answers will vary; the route was long and passed through many western states.

Find the Main Idea and Details, p. 43

Underline the first sentence.

1. Indians and fur trappers used it for hunting and trade.
2. Missionaries used it to reach Indians they could convert.
3. Farmers used it to get to free land in Oregon.

4. Miners used it to reach California.

Underline the last sentence.

5. Travelers needed to gather firewood and find fresh water.
6. Wagons needed to be repaired.
7. Meals had to be cooked over open fires.
8. Settlers had to unpack and repack wagons each day as they set up camp.

Check Your Comprehension, p. 45

1. The trip became faster, easier, and cheaper.
2. the Union Pacific Railroad and the Central Pacific Railroad
3. *Sample answer:* The Union Pacific built more miles of track than the Central Pacific.

Practice Finding the Main Idea and Details, p. 45

1. Native Americans were a challenge for the railroad.
2. Native Americans viewed the railroad as a threat.
3. They attacked workers.
4. They tore up track.
5. They stole things.
6. The Chinese were treated poorly and unfairly by the railroad.
7. The Chinese had the most dangerous jobs.
8. They were paid less than white workers.
9. They worked longer hours in harsh conditions.
10. They were whipped.
   Many Chinese workers died.

Respond to the Readings, p. 46

1. Travelers had to buy a wagon and the animals to pull it as well as all the supplies for the journey.
2. Travelers had difficult work, they had to cross dangerous lands, and they faced harsh weather conditions. They didn't have medical care or doctors if they were sick or injured.
3. a
4. It was easier to lay track on the flat land. In the mountains, the

weather was cold and tunnels had to be blasted through rock.

5. The Union Pacific and the Central Pacific Railroads each faced challenges as they built a railroad to join the eastern U.S. to the west.
6. Both the trail and the railroad gave people a way to reach western lands to settle.

Use Word Parts, p. 46

Definitions will vary; sample definitions:

1. a shy person; a person who turns within
2. a friendly person who likes being with others
3. turned back
4. to turn or change direction
5. turn upside down

Review the Vocabulary, p. 47

1. b
2. c
3. c
4. a
5. pursued
6. section
7. progress
8. doubted
9. converted
10. establish
11–12. Sentences will vary.

LESSON 5

Vocabulary Tip, p. 51

1. people don't understand the process, don't have enough money saved, or have a low credit score
2. Answers will vary.

Check Your Comprehension, p. 53

1. It gave African American men the right to vote.
2. A poll tax was an annual fee people had to pay before they could vote.
3. Text 2 tells why voting is important and what African American men needed to do in order to vote.

Analyze Purpose and Point of View, p. 53

1. b
2. poll taxes and literacy tests
3. Only 6% of black men were registered to vote in Mississippi.
4. a
5. opinion
6. Voting is how you choose the people who will be in control of your interests.
7. It tells about the things you should do in order to be able to vote and serve the interests of your state and the nation.
8. b
9. to persuade them to vote

Check Your Comprehension, p. 55

1. The author wants to give women the right to vote by passing the suffrage amendment.
2. The author thinks women do not need to vote.
3. Since women work, fight, and die alongside men, they should be allowed to vote alongside men.

Practice Analyzing Purpose and Point of View, p. 55

Answers may vary. Sample answers given.

1. a list of reasons why women should be given the right to vote
2. The author wants readers to understand why women should vote. The author names other countries that have given women the right to vote; the author explains that women helped win the war and that women's suffrage is part of human freedom.
3. The author has a positive view about women voting. The author believes the suffrage amendment should be passed.
4. tips, advice, and reasons why women do not need to vote
5. The author wants readers to understand that women do not need to vote in order to have a happy and well-run home. The author thinks voting will do more harm than good. The

author gives statistics to show women don't want or care to vote and will not be effective voters anyway.

6. The author has a negative view of women's suffrage. The author thinks it will be harmful.
7. The information is presented as a cartoon drawing.
8. The author wants viewers to see that men will have to do the work women used to do. It's supported by showing a man washing clothes, wearing an apron, and watching the baby.
9. The author has a negative view of women's suffrage. The author thinks suffrage will be harmful to the home and family.

Respond to the Readings, p. 56

1. White officials could choose difficult passages for African Americans to interpret and could decide who passed and failed.
2. The rules required people to live in Mississippi for two years, pay a poll tax, and pass a literacy test. Many people couldn't read, and those who could might be given an unfair test. Because only 6% of black men were registered to vote in Mississippi, it is clear it was difficult to meet all the rules.
3. They both use the idea that women should get the vote because they have worked to help win a war.
4. The author of Text 3 sees voting as a human freedom that women have earned and that other countries have already granted. The author of Text 4 sees women's suffrage as unnecessary and potentially harmful and dangerous.
5. Answers will vary.

Use Word Parts, p. 56

1. international
2. internet
3. interrupt
4. interact
5. interpreter
6. interfere

7. interstate
8. intermission

Review the Vocabulary, p. 57

1. cooperation
2. allow
3. emphasize
4. barrier
5. consistent
6. interpret
7. denied
8. influence
9. competition
10. eligible
11–12. Sentences will vary.

LESSON 6

Vocabulary Tip, p. 61

1. c
2. b
3. a

Check Your Comprehension, p. 63

1. Foods in short supply were rationed, such as sugar, meat, cheese, butter, and canned food.
2. A victory garden was a family or community garden where people grew their own vegetables.
3. Children organized metal drives in their neighborhoods to collect old toys, pots and pans, and even bottle caps.

Make Inferences, p. 63

1. X
2. I
3. I
4. X
5. I
6. I
7. X
8. I

Check Your Comprehension, p. 65

1. Philip Johnston came up with the idea of using the Navajo language as the basis for a code.
2. The Navajo language had no written form and was spoken by very few people who weren't Navajo.
3. They learned to use radio and telephone equipment.

Practice Making Inferences, p. 65

Answers may vary.

Respond to the Readings, p. 66

1. The war effort was all the work people did and the sacrifices they made on the home front to support the war.

2. They were needed to make things needed in the war, including weapons.

3. It explains that it made it harder to break the code.

4. Code talkers did general Marine duties, operated and maintained radio and telephone equipment, and transmitted critical communications in code quickly and accurately.

5. Answers will vary.

Use Word Parts, p. 66

1. active
2. appreciative
3. attractive
4. cooperative
5. creative
6. decisive
7. effective
8. expensive
9. effective
10. creative
11. cooperative
12. active

13–14. Answers will vary.

Review the Vocabulary, p. 67

1. critical
2. extensive
3. represent
4. distribute
5. weapons
6. code
7. fluent
8. effort
9. encourage
10. sacrifices

Unit 2 Review, p. 70

1. c
2. d
3. a

4. b

UNIT 3
LESSON 7

Vocabulary Tip, p. 73

1. c
2. d
3. a
4. b

Check Your Comprehension, p. 75

1. It was a disease that killed millions of people in Europe in the mid-1300s.

2. It arrived on a trading ship in Messina on the island of Sicily.

3. *Possible answer:* The map shows that bubonic plague spread inland and northward over time.

Synthesize, p. 75

1. They got lumps, black spots, fever, vomiting, and pain.

2. Most died within a few days.

3. There were a lot of dead bodies, and families couldn't bury relatives on their own. It was common to see death.

4. *Possible answer:* The disease struck and killed so many that it had a huge impact on the world's population.

5. It spread along trade routes.

6. Trading ships that came to a port on Sicily carried the plague.

7. *Possible answer:* Trade in the 1300s contributed not just to the movement of goods, but spread the plague.

8. The plague was spread mostly by rats and fleas.

9. Rats liked to live on ships and in towns, which were filthy.

10. *Possible answer:* The use of ships for trade and the dirty conditions in towns helped infected rats and fleas spread the disease more widely.

Check Your Comprehension, p. 77

1. It is about a flu pandemic.

2. U.S. soldiers were sent to Europe and some carried the flu virus with them.

3. *Possible answers:* It encourages people to wear a mask.

Practice Synthesizing, p. 77

1. The flu spread rapidly at a military training camp; it killed mostly young adults.

2. *Possible answer:* Conditions at the training camp might have made it easy for flu to spread among young adults.

3. Flu spreads in droplets from coughs and sneezes; large numbers of troops went to Europe carrying the flu with them.

4. *Possible answer:* Wartime conditions meant people were moving around the world. Conditions in the trenches made it easier for flu to spread rapidly.

5. A second, deadlier wave of flu broke out at a U.S. military base. Medical staff were overwhelmed. There was a lack of medical staff. Censorship limited how much people knew.

6. *Possible answer:* Treating the flu was made more difficult because so many people were close together at military bases, there weren't enough resources because of the war, and the public lacked information.

7. *Possible answer:* Movement of troops and conditions at military bases and battle during World War I may have contributed to the flu pandemic. The war also made it harder for the flu to be treated and addressed.

Respond to the Readings, p. 78

1. c

2. It created ugly black spots on people, it killed a lot of people, and people didn't understand what caused it.

3. It killed 50 million to 100 million people in just 15 months, and it killed young adults.

4. Military training camps had a lot of people crowded together in a small amount of space, so it was easy to transmit the virus. Soldiers at war lived in cramped conditions and were weakened

from battle, which may have made it easier for them to get sick.

5. *Possible answers:* Both killed a lot of people in a short amount of time; both spread as people moved around the world; doctors were unable to cure the illnesses or stop their spread.

Use Word Parts, p. 78

1. biosphere
2. biohazard
3. biographer
4. biology
5. autobiography
6. biodiversity

Review the Vocabulary, p. 79

1. thrive
2. report
3. origin
4. rapid
5. symptom
6. appear
7. realize
8. residents
9. overwhelmed
10. contagious

LESSON 8

Vocabulary Tip, p. 83

d

Check Your Comprehension, p. 85

1. Invasive species adapt easily to their new home, spread, and cause harm.
2. They can be brought on purpose, or they arrive by accident, coming on cargo ships, for example.
3. Pythons were brought to the U.S. as pets. Hogs were brought by settlers.

Compare and Contrast, p. 85

1. wheat, apples, cattle, honeybees
2. invasive species
3. the environment and the economy
4. different, Similarly, also
5. They were all brought to the U.S. on purpose.

6. They arrived by accident on cargo ships.
7. *Possible answer:* both animals were brought on purpose; both are invasive; both have thrived; both lack natural predators.
8. *Possible answers:* Burmese pythons are reptiles, but pigs are mammals; pythons were brought as pets, but pigs were brought as food; pythons live in warm swampy areas, but wild hogs can live in many conditions.
9. There are many more wild hogs than Burmese pythons.
10. Wild hogs; they live in 39 states, while the pythons live in just 1.

Check Your Comprehension, p. 87

1. They cause economic harm, spread disease, and hurt ecosystems.
2. Fire ants mainly harm people and animals and long-horned beetles harm trees.
3. The maps help you understand where each insect lives now and where it might spread to in the future.

Practice Comparing and Contrasting, p. 87

1. hurt people and animals
2. from South America
3–5. *Possible answers:* were imported by accident; invasive insects; came on a ship; potential to spread
6. large size, 20–35 mm
7. came in 1996
8. affects mainly northeastern states
9. *Possible answer:* Contrasting. Although both are invasive insects, they cause different types of damage, affect different parts of the country, and behave very differently.

Respond to the Readings, p. 88

1. They don't have any predators to control their numbers, and they reduce populations of native wildlife.

2. They are able to easily adapt to many different conditions in the U.S., and they reproduce rapidly.
3. Both red imported fire ants and Asian long-horned beetles are invasive insects that can cause big problems.
4. *Possible answer:* There would probably be an economic impact if trees used for lumber are killed. There could be an environmental impact, too, if animals that depend on trees or forests lose their habitats.
5. Answers will vary.

Use Word Parts, p. 88

1. erupts
2. interruptions
3. abrupt
4. bankrupt
5. rupture
6. corrupt
7–8. Sentences will vary.

Review the Vocabulary, p. 89

1. c
2. c
3. b
4. a
5. potential
6. disturb
7. decline
8. intentional
9. disrupt
10. impact

LESSON 9

Vocabulary Tip, p. 93

d

Check Your Comprehension, p. 95

1. The droughts began in 1930.
2. Black Sunday was April 14, 1935, the worst black blizzard of the Dust Bowl era.
3. The map shows the states that were affected by the Dust Bowl.

Identify Sequence, p. 95

1. **a.** 4
   b. 2
   c. 1

ANSWER KEY

d. 3

2. *Answers will vary. Possible answers:*
   a. There were four severe droughts on the Great Plains during the 1930s.
   b. The droughts killed the crops.
   c. High winds picked up the soil and blew it into dust storms.

3. *Answers will vary. Possible answers:*
   a. Large dust storms, called "black blizzards" would sweep up millions of tons of dirt from the dry fields and swirl it up into the air.
   b. April 14, 1935, known as "Black Sunday," was the worst black blizzard of the Dirty '30s. More than 300,000 tons of dust traveled across the country to the East Coast.

Check Your Comprehension, p. 97

1. Another name for a mudslide is a "debris flow."

2. Mudslides are most likely to occur on the hillsides of the West Coast.

3. A burn scar is where the ground is so burnt that the soil cannot absorb the rain.

Practice Identifying Sequence, p. 97

1. **a.** 4
   b. 3
   c. 1
   d. 2

2. *Answers will vary. Possible answers:*
   Roads and buildings are built or logging has occurred.
   ⇩
   Natural disaster occurs, such as earthquake or wild fire.
   ⇩
   Wildfires cause burn scars and soil can no longer absorb rain.
   ⇩
   It rains.
   ⇩
   Debris flow occurs.

Respond to the Readings, p. 98

1. The Dust Bowl took place in North Dakota, South Dakota, Nebraska, Kansas, Oklahoma, Texas, New Mexico, Colorado, Wyoming, and Montana.

2. *Answers will vary. Possible answer:* Abandoned fields and land that had been cleared of grass were very dry because of years of drought. This caused the Dust Bowl when high winds blew in.

3. Mudslides are landslides made of mud.

4. *Answers will vary. Possible answer:* Rain soaks the dry soil. The water works in between the grains of soil. Boulders, trees, and other debris are pushed free. The debris accumulates and slides downhill.

5. Answers will vary.

Use Word Parts, p. 98

1. brighten
2. darken
3. frighten
4. loosen
5. shorten
6. straighten
7. sweeten
8. worsen
9. loosen
10. sweeten
11. brighten
12. frighten
13. darken
14. shorten

Review the Vocabulary, p. 99

1. absorb
2. swirl
3. collapse
4. disaster
5. region
6. decade
7. drought
8. abandon
9. accumulate
10. prone to

Unit 3 Review, p. 102

1. b
2. d
3. a
4. d

UNIT 4
LESSON 10
Vocabulary Tip, p. 105

1. c
2. a
3. b

Check Your Comprehension, p. 107

1. This part of the story takes place in an open boat on the ocean.

2. The characters include the cook, the oiler, the reporter, and the captain.

3. It describes the struggle the boat faces battling the waves.

Understand Figurative Language and Imagery, p. 107

1. They were only looking at the waves around them.

2. The horizon seems to get wider and narrower and to move up and down.

3. rocks

4. c

5. a bathtub

6. The boat is very small.

7. Sitting in the boat was like sitting on a bucking bronco.

8. *Possible answers:* pranced, reared, plunged, leaping, scramble, bumping, race

9. The next menace is the next wave; each wave is a threat or danger.

10. *Possible answers:* anxious, outburst, effort, grim, grace, snarling

Check Your Comprehension, p. 109

1. Gulls and seaweed are also floating on the ocean.

2. They're rowing a lot.

3. The men see a lighthouse in the distance.

ANSWER KEY

Practice Understanding Figurative Language and Imagery, p. 109

1. The words help show that the sea is rough and violent toward the men.
2. b
3. carpets on a clothesline; islands
4. The gulls sit comfortably and don't feel the sea's anger.
5. The men in the boat must struggle against the sea, but the birds and seaweed are at ease.
6. It looks like the point of a pin.
7. The lighthouse looks so small because it is very far away.
8–10. *Answers will vary. Possible answers:* the waves are jagged and form points like rocks; the waves are abrupt and tall; being in the boat is like being on a bucking bronco; the boat is leaping in the air and splashing down; the waves are a menace; the waves keep coming; the waves are walls of water; the waves are like hills; the spray from waves slashes past the men.
11. *Possible answer:* The sea is harsh and violent and does not care about the men in the boat.

Respond to the Readings, p. 110

1. c
2. The men in the boat don't think the view is splendid or glorious because they are struggling to survive, but someone not in the boat would probably see the beauty.
3. More realistic; the events are things that could really occur, and the men act in the ways real people would act.
4. Answers will vary.
5. Answers will vary.

Use Word Parts, p. 110

1. surcharge
2. surface
3. supersize
4. surplus
5. supervises
6. surpassed

7–8. Sentences will vary.

Review the Vocabulary, p. 111

1. a
2. b
3. c
4. a
5. c
6. c
7. abrupt
8. outburst
9. comfortably
10. grim

LESSON 11

Vocabulary Tip, p. 115

1. c.
2. *Clue:* made into newspapers

Check Your Comprehension, p. 117

1. Johnsy is counting the leaves left on the vine.
2. Sue is Johnsy's roommate and friend. She's also an artist.
3. Behrman is a failed artist who lives on the ground floor.

Analyze Characters, p. 117

1. She has made up her mind that she's not going to get well.
2. She's very upset with the doctor's news.
3. "When the last one falls I must go, too."
4. She thinks it's nonsense and that leaves have nothing to do with Johnsy getting well.
5. She says she won't be gone a minute.
6. He had never been successful as an artist and never painted the masterpiece he still spoke of. He had stopped painting and liked to drink.

Check Your Comprehension, p. 119

1. She had been up painting Behrman all night.
2. She realized it is wrong to want to die.
3. He painted a leaf on the wall so that Johnsy wouldn't give up.

Practice Analyzing Character, p. 119

1–8. Answers will vary.

Respond to the Readings, p. 120

1. Johnsy has made up her mind that she's not going to get well. If she doesn't want to live, medicine is powerless.
2. That Johnsy will die when the last leaf falls.
3. To model so she can paint him.
4. She asks for some soup and talks about painting in Italy someday.

Use Word Parts, p. 120

1. j
2. f
3. g
4. h
5. i
6. a
7. b
8. e
9. c
10. d
11. nonstop
12. nonflammable
13. nondescript
14. nonprofit

Review the Vocabulary, p. 121

1. a
2. c
3. a
4. c
5. persistent
6. nonsense
7. scarcely
8. pneumonia
9. dreadful
10. pulp

LESSON 12

Vocabulary Tip, p. 125

1. *Possible answers:* to tear into bite-sized pieces, gulp
2. to eat quickly

Check Your Comprehension, p. 127

1. Zomo, Sky God, Big Fish, Wild Cow, Leopard
2. Zomo wants Sky God to give him wisdom.

3. He must get scales from Big Fish, milk from Big Cow, and a tooth from Leopard.

Understand a Story's Theme, p. 127

1. Zomo wants wisdom from Sky God.

2. Zomo's cleverness helps him get scales from Big Fish. This tells me Zomo really is as clever as he thinks.

3. To get a tooth from Leopard, Zomo uses both cleverness and speed. This tells me he is good at making decisions quickly.

4. Sky God tells him that in order to be wise he must also use caution. In completing the tasks, Zomo was not very cautious.

5. Zomo knows he is wise at the end of the story because he demonstrated caution by running away from danger.

6. *Possible answer:* Zomo has wisdom at the end of the story because he has all the traits Sky God says he needs.

7. b

Check Your Comprehension, p. 129

1. This story's main characters are the magpie, the fox, and the quail.

2. The fox tricks the magpie into giving him two of her chicks.

3. The quail helps the magpie by telling her not to give the fox any more chicks and then by feeding the fox herself.

Practice Understanding a Story's Theme, p. 129

1. the magpie, the fox, the quail

2. The fox has eaten some of the magpie's chicks.

3. The quail helps the magpie by feeding the fox rice, but after three days, she gets tired of working so hard and being taken advantage of.

4. The fox is punished by being killed.

5. The lesson is don't take advantage of others.

Respond to the Readings, p. 130

1. These tasks would be impossible for a rabbit—unless he was as clever as Zomo.

2. He snatched the tooth out of Leopard's paw.

3. The quail solves the problem by tricking the hunter into killing the fox.

4. Answers will vary.

5. *Possible answer:* The quail in "The Magpie and the Fox" is most like Zomo because both of these characters trick others to accomplish their goals.

Use Word Parts, p. 130

1. to create a circle around something

2. to seal something inside an envelope

3. to put information into a coded form

4. to put something inside of a case

5. in danger or at risk

6. to imagine or picture

Review the Vocabulary, p. 131

1. evade
2. refuse
3. entice
4. devour
5. caution
6. devise
7. resist
8. wisdom
9. clever
10. implement

Unit 4 Review, p. 134

1. d
2. a
3. b
4. a

LANGUAGE SKILLS MINI-LESSONS

Sentence Fragments, p. 135

Sentences will vary. Sample sentences shown.

1. F; My brother goes to work at the store at 10 p.m. and stays until 6 a.m.

2. F; Fresh produce near the front of the store helps make shoppers buy more food.

3. S

4. S

5. F; Fruits and vegetables, meat, fish, eggs, and dairy products are usually on the perimeter of the store.

6. F; The average shopper spends a little over three minutes waiting to check out.

7. S

8. F; The samples of food that some stores give shoppers are tasty.

Frequently Confused Words, p. 136

1. accept, a; except, b
2. advice, b; advise, a
3. affect, a; effect b
4. already, a; all ready, b
5. loose, b; lose, a
6. maybe, a; may be: b
7. weather, a; whether, b
8. whose, b; who's, a
9. whether
10. Maybe
11. advice
12. Whose
13. effect

Capitalization, p. 137

1. Ms. Jane Franklin
2. (none)
3. Europe
4. Santa Fe Trail
5. (none)
6. Mississippi River
7. *Call of the Wild*, by Jack London
8. The book *Little House on the Prairie* was written by Laura Ingalls Wilder.
9. Many soldiers who fought in the Civil War got jobs with the Union Pacific Railroad.
10. The Oregon Trail went from Independence, Missouri, to Oregon City, Oregon.

11. Travelers stopped at Fort Kearney and then followed the Platte River.
12. Many Chinese immigrants came to the United States during the California Gold Rush.
13. Marcus and Narcissa Whitman were missionaries who wanted to convert the Cayuse Indians.

Shifts in Tense, p. 138

1. Millions of families <u>planted</u> Victory Gardens and grew their own vegetables.
2. Food rationing began in 1942 and <u>continued</u> for a year after the war.
3. c
4. c
5. Rationing books <u>had</u> deadlines for when you could use the stamps.
6. has, are
7. grew up, spoke
8. believed, was, proved, was
9. c
10. a

Commas, p. 139

1. Because of censorship during the war, newspapers were not allowed to report on flu outbreaks.
2. Bubonic plague first came to Europe at the port of Messina, Sicily.
3. During the second wave of the flu, there was an outbreak near Boston, Massachusetts, that soon spread to other places.

4. Doctors, nurses, and other medical workers became sick while treating flu patients.
5. In just a few years, about one-third of the world's population died from bubonic plague.
6. No commas needed.
7. The flu spread rapidly, and people weren't sure how to stop it.
8. To stop the spread of the flu, officials closed schools, churches, and theaters.
9. When soldiers were sent to fight in World War I, they carried the flu with them.
10. Some of the symptoms of plague included black spots on skin, fever, vomiting, and lumps.
11. No commas needed.
12. Past outbreaks of flu had killed mainly young, old, or sick people.
13. No commas needed.

Conditionals, p. 140

1. a
2. a
3. c
4. d
5. keeps
6. wouldn't have written
7. would read
8. hadn't been
9. blew

Run-On Sentences, p. 141

1. Tuesdays are the worst day to ride the bus. It is very crowded.

2. correct
3. Marco drives to class. He parks in the lot on First Street.
4. I can't use my cell phone. The battery level is too low.
5. The test was very hard, but Linda got an A.
6. The room is small and dark, so Tina wants to paint it a bright color.
7. Fred will go to truck driving school, or he will sign up for college classes.
8. The basketball game was exciting, and the team made some amazing shots.

Commas and Quotation Marks, p. 142

1. "If she were interested in the future, her chances would be better," said the doctor.
2. Sue answered, "She always wanted to paint in Italy."
3. "I want to see the last leaf fall," explained Johnsy. "I have done enough waiting."
4. "I'm going to close the blind," said Sue. "I don't want you to look at those leaves."
5. "Try to sleep," whispered Sue. She closed the door behind her.
6. Behrman cried, "That poor little Johnsy!"
7. "She is very sick and weak," said Sue.
8. Behrman replied, "Someday I will paint my masterpiece."
9. correct